CAROLINE COX · ROBERT BALCHIN · JOHN MARKS

CHOOSING A
STATE
SCHOOL

Caroline Cox was head of the Sociology Department at the Polytechnic of North London and then Director of the Nursing Education Research Unit at Chelsea College, University of London. She writes and lectures widely about education and was created a Life Peer in 1982. She has three children, all of whom were educated at a comprehensive school.

Robert Balchin has been a teacher in most kinds of school and was the headmaster of an independent school for nine years. A former county councillor who has been a governor of five local authority schools, he is presently a company director and the Director-General of St John Ambulance. He has twin sons of thirteen.

John Marks has taught at a direct grant school and has lectured at London University and in Sweden. Until recently a senior lecturer in the School of Applied Physics at the Polytechnic of North London, he is now a director of the Educational Research Trust. He has three children, all educated at their local comprehensive school, of which he is an elected parent governor.

CAROLINE COX · ROBERT BALCHIN · JOHN MARKS

CHOOSING A STATE SCHOOL

How to find the best education for your child

HUTCHINSON PRESS

LONDON · SYDNEY · AUCKLAND · JOHANNESBURG

First published in 1989 by Century Hutchinson Ltd,
Brookmount House, 62–65 Chandos Place, London WC2N 4NW

Century Hutchinson Group (Australia) Pty Ltd
88–91 Albion Street, Surry Hills, NSW 2010

Century Hutchinson Group (NZ) Ltd
32–34 View Road, PO Box 40-086, Glenfield, Auckland 10

Century Hutchinson Group (SA) Pty Ltd
PO Box 337, Bergvlei 2012, South Africa

Cover design by Shireen Nathoo

This book was designed and produced by
Pardoe Blacker Limited, East Grinstead, Sussex

Set in Monotype Rockwell by Southern Positives and Negatives (SPAN),
Lingfield, Surrey

Printed and bound in Great Britain by Purnell Book Production Ltd

ISBN 0-09-174071-1

Contents

How to use this book *page* 7
Abbreviations used in the book 8

Introduction 9

Chapter One: Know your rights 11
The right to choose. The right to information. The right to appeal. Other rights: free transport; special needs.

FACT PANELS: 1. Your local eduction authority 12
2. The different types of state-maintained schools 14
3. The independent schools 16
4. Information available from schools 19
5. Information available from your local education authority 20
6. The standard number and school rolls (Education Reform Act 1988) 21
7. Special schools 24

Chapter Two: Choosing a primary school 25
Reading the prospectus. Looking at the school from the outside. Visiting the school. Making your final choice.

Chapter Three: The General Certificate of Secondary Education 33
FACT PANEL: 8. A guide to the examination system 34

Chapter Four: Choosing a secondary school 37
Obtaining information about examination results. Two neighbouring schools. Comparing schools in your area. Comparing your results with the national benchmarks. Comparing advanced level results. A look at other types of schools. Making use of the tables.

Chapter Five: Choosing a secondary school: what else to look for 61
Reading the prospectus. Looking at the school from outside. Visiting the school. Making your final choice.

Chapter Six: How to change schools 72

Chapter Seven: How your local education authority can help you 73

Good practice. Ideal practice

FACT PANEL: Assisted places scheme 75

Conclusion 77

A compendium of helpful information 79

SECTION ONE: Choosing at sixteen 80

SECTION TWO: Information for parents living in Scotland 82

SECTION THREE: Information for parents living in Northern Ireland 84

SECTION FOUR: The assisted places scheme: schools participating in England, Wales and Scotland 85

SECTION FIVE: Relevant sections from the Education Act 1980, the Education (No 2) Act 1986 and the Education Reform Act 1988 92

SECTION SIX: Addresses of local education authorities 104

SECTION SEVEN: Some useful addresses 112

SECTION EIGHT: A guide to career requirements 113

Index 167

How to use this book

Most of the help and advice in this book is for those whose children are either going to school for the first time or moving up to a secondary school. It also offers, however, a useful guide for those who, at any time, are dissatisfied with their children's schooling and are considering a transfer, or for those who have moved house and are searching for a new school.

The information is of two sorts: there is a clear step-by-step guide to choosing a school (useful for both the state and private sectors) and there are fact panels, examination benchmark tables and sections which provide valuable additional material to assist parents when they are making their choice.

We recommend that you read through the main guide quickly and then work through it again. This time use the fact panels and the tables to help you take practical steps, such as sending for school prospectuses and comparing them systematically.

Chapter Four explains how to use the *national benchmark figures* to compare examination results for the schools you are considering. Tables 9 to 17 on pages 52 to 60 have spaces provided so that you can insert examination results for your neighbourhood schools in order to see how they measure up to each other and to the national benchmarks. These benchmarks do not apply to the Scottish Certificate of Education.

THE COMPENDIUM OF HELPFUL INFORMATION contains sections giving guidance for those whose children have reached the official school-leaving age, information for those living in Scotland and Northern Ireland, details of those schools participating in the assisted places scheme and lists of addresses of local education authorities and other addresses. The relevant sections of the 1980, 1986 and 1988 Education Acts are there to help you back up your requests for information from your local education authority, if this is not readily forthcoming. The last section provides a CAREERS GUIDE giving the basic academic requirements for each job, so that your child's aspirations and aptitude may be taken into consideration when you are choosing a school with strengths in particular departments.

Abbreviations used in the book

A-level	advanced level GCE
APS	assisted places scheme
CPVE	Certificate of Prevocational Education
CSE	Certificate of Secondary Education
CTC	City Technology College
DES	Department of Education and Science
FE	further education
GCE	General Certificate of Education
GCSE	General Certificate of Secondary Education
ILEA	Inner London Education Authority
LEA	local education authority
MSC	Manpower Services Commission
O-level	ordinary level GCE
PCAS	Polytechnic Central Admissions System
SCE	Scottish Certificate of Education
TVEI	Technical and Vocational Education Initiative
UCCA	Universities Central Council on Admissions
YTS	Youth Training Scheme

Introduction

The school that your child attends for the next few years will play an important part in shaping the rest of his or her life. There will be a number of schools to choose from in your area, but how do you go about finding the best one amongst them for your son or daughter?

The world of education is specialized and complicated and most parents have had little experience of it since the day they left school themselves. How can you tell if a school is the best one and the one most likely to provide the kind of education which will be the basis for a good career?

Many factors make up a good school. We mention most of them in the following pages but, of course, not every school can excel at everything. Research shows, however, that there are significant differences among schools, even those in the same neighbourhoods and especially in big cities. The aim of this book is to help you identify these differences. It describes the kinds of education which you may find locally and your legal rights as a parent to information about schools. It indicates what you should look for when you visit a school, and shows you how to appeal if your child is not awarded a place at the school of your first choice.

The results of external examinations, such as GCSE, are very valuable objective indicators of the standards of a secondary school. They are one amongst a number of criteria on which a school's success can be judged, and we offer others. We believe, however, that it is extremely important to bear examination results in mind when you are choosing a school.

This book is unique in providing parents, for the first time, with a simple and trustworthy method of comparing examination results. Using it, a parent can compare the local school's figures, not just with those of neighbouring schools, but also with the national benchmarks for that type of school. National benchmarks are the national average number of passes per fifth-year pupil for all schools of a particular type. They are given subject by subject and from them you can easily see how, for instance, a school's mathematics department measures up to those in similar schools elsewhere.

The national benchmarks are based on some highly original research. After the 1980 Education Act all state schools were required to begin publishing their examination results, something which only a minority had done before. In an extensive project which involved sending for statistics from thousands of schools, Caroline Cox and John Marks produced, for the very first time, an analysis of this country's examination results. A prolonged critical appraisal by the statisticians of the Department of Education and Science confirmed their findings.

Another result of the 1980 Education Act was to give parents a far greater measure of choice among state schools than ever before and to oblige all schools to publish prospectuses containing useful information on which parents can base that choice. Before the Act, parents were often directed to use a particular school or had to plump for a school without knowing very much about it.

Remember that it is now government policy that parents should have a much greater say in the education of their children; in effect, as ratepayers and taxpayers, parents are 'customers' of the education service.

We hope that you will find help and advice in this book and with it you will be able to make an informed choice among the schools in your locality. It is worth making the effort; after all, schooldays, once gone, cannot be repeated and you will want to ensure that your child receives the best possible education from them.

RGAB

Know your rights

You have a number of rights when choosing a school for your child. These are established by the Education Act 1980. In particular the Act provides three basic parental rights:

☐ the right to choose which school you want your child to attend
☐ the right to information which will enable you to choose the most appropriate school for your child
☐ the right to appeal if your choice of school is not upheld.

Many local education authorities (LEAs) are exemplary in fulfilling all these rights. The information they give is comprehensive and easily available. Many are helpful and considerate in meeting parents' educational choices for their children. Others, however, do not have such a good reputation. If you are not sure of your rights, or have been frustrated in your attempts to get information, or unable to secure the best possible education for your child, this chapter gives guidelines on how you can change the situation and play a more positive role in determining your child's future.

The right to choose

Strictly speaking, you do not have an absolute right to determine to which school your child will go. However, the 1980 Education Act provides that you have the right to express a preference and to state why, and that this preference *must* be met by your LEA, unless it has some good reason why it cannot comply. Obviously, any outstandingly good school will attract pupils and may have only sufficient space to hold applicants from its own immediate neighbourhood (catchment area). All parents, of course, want their children to go to the best school in the locality.

If, after careful assessment of the schools in your area, you do not think there is an appropriate school for your child, you are entitled to request a place at a school outside your county or LEA district, stating the reasons for your choice. You may have a strong preference for a school employing particular teaching methods or providing special subjects. You may prefer a single-sex school, or a certain denominational attitude. Your child may wish to pursue a specific career or may be gifted in a field best suited to a particular school, or there may be medical reasons for your choice.

Whatever the reasons, the other LEA, or in the case of a voluntary-aided school, the board of governors, must consider your child. If he or she is accepted for schooling by another county or district, your LEA will pay the other LEA, within the terms of the 1980 Education Act.

The 1980 Education Act provides LEAs with the right to refuse a parent's choice 'if the provision of efficient education or the efficient use of resources is prejudiced'. Do note that herein lies the basis for much of the misunderstanding between parents and LEAs. This provision is open to interpretation, of course, but very often merely means that where a school is over-subscribed, the LEA need not comply with your request, claiming that 'efficient education is prejudiced'. For instance, few LEAs will agree to pay the fees in whole or in part, should you choose an independent school for your child. They will not deem this an 'efficient use of resources'. If there are grammar or other selective schools in your area, your child may legitimately be refused a place on the basis of failure to pass an entrance test. Places at independent schools are available under the government's assisted places scheme (APS), which is not funded by your LEA and therefore not governed by its rules. Any reasonable preference *must* be met, and many LEAs will do this automatically, or you may come to an agreement after an informal discussion with your local education officer. But some LEAs may not make this so easy for you, so be sure of your rights and, firmly and politely , stick to them. Do not be fobbed off with the nearest school unless you are sure it is the right one for your child.

FACT PANEL 1

Your local education authority (LEA)

Your local education authority is normally the local council to which you pay your rates. If you live in the country, this will be one of the thirty-nine English or eight Welsh county councils. If you live in a town, your LEA is probably one of the fifty-six borough councils. For those who live in one of the twelve boroughs in central London your LEA is currently the Inner London Education Authority (ILEA). From 1st April 1990, however, the ILEA will cease to exist and responsibility for education will be transferred to the twelve London boroughs.

A map showing the distribution of the local education authorities is given opposite.

1 **Cornwall**
2 **Devon**
3 **Dorset**
4 **Isle of Wight**
5 **Hampshire**
6 **Surrey**
7 **West Sussex**
8 **East Sussex**
9 **Kent**
10 **ILEA**
11 **London:** Barking, Barnet, Bexley, Brent, Bromley, Croydon, Ealing, Enfield, Haringey, Harrow, Havering, Hillingdon, Hounslow, Kingston upon Thames, Merton, Newham, Redbridge, Richmond upon Thames, Sutton, Waltham Forest
12 **Berkshire**
13 **Wiltshire**
14 **Somerset**
15 **Avon**
16 **Gloucestershire**
17 **Oxfordshire**
18 **Buckinghamshire**
19 **Hertfordshire**
20 **Essex**
21 **Suffolk**
22 **Cambridgeshire**

23 **Bedfordshire**
24 **Northamptonshire**
25 **Warwickshire**
26 **Hereford and Worcester**
27 **Gwent**
28 **South Glamorgan**
29 **Mid Glamorgan**
30 **West Glamorgan**
31 **Dyfed**
32 **Powys**
33 **Shropshire**
34 **West Midlands:** Birmingham, Coventry, Dudley, Sandwell, Solihull, Walsall, Wolverhampton
35 **Leicestershire**
36 **Norfolk**
37 **Lincolnshire**
38 **Nottinghamshire**

39 **Derbyshire**
40 **Staffordshire**
41 **Cheshire**
42 **Clwyd**
43 **Gwynedd**
44 **Merseyside:** Knowsley, Liverpool, St Helens, Sefton, Wirral
45 **Greater Manchester:** Bolton, Bury, Manchester, Oldham, Rochdale, Salford, Stockport, Tameside, Trafford, Wigan
46 **West Yorkshire:** Bradford, Calderdale, Kirklees, Leeds, Wakefield
47 **South Yorkshire:** Barnsley, Doncaster, Rotherham, Sheffield
48 **Humberside**
49 **North Yorkshire**
50 **Lancashire**
51 **Cumbria**
52 **Durham**
53 **Cleveland**
54 **Tyne and Wear:** Gateshead, Newcastle upon Tyne, North Tyneside, South Tyneside, Sunderland
55 **Northumberland**

For addresses of local education authorities see pages 104–111.

You have a choice, when you send your child to a school within the state system, amongst county schools or voluntary-aided or voluntary-controlled schools. Definitions and information about the various types of school are given in Fact Panels 2 and 3. Briefly, county schools are the most common types of school and are wholly maintained by the local education authority. Voluntary-aided and voluntary-controlled schools are usually owned by the churches, but maintained by the LEAs.

FACT PANEL 2

The different types of state-maintained schools

COUNTY SCHOOLS

These schools are wholly maintained by the LEA, and are the most common type of school. They include:

Primary schools. This is a general term for schools that cater for children between the ages of five and eleven. Most of them tend to take pupils from their immediate neighbourhoods. Schools for children between five and eight are usually called *infant schools*. Those for children between eight and eleven are usually known as *junior schools*. In areas where there are *middle schools*, schools for five- to nine-year-olds are generally known as *first schools*.

Secondary schools. These are for children from the age of eleven upwards. They may be further subdivided into various types of school, not all of which may be represented in your area, such as:

Comprehensive schools. These are the most common type of secondary school, and aim to admit pupils across the whole academic ability range. Many of them tend to take their pupils from their immediate neighbourhoods, often called the catchment area.

Grammar schools. These are for pupils whose academic abilities are considerably above average. Only a minority of LEAs now have grammar schools. In the few remaining areas where all the schools are selective, approximately 25 per cent of pupils are selected for grammar schools.

Secondary modern schools. These admit pupils of average, and below average, academic ability. Only a minority of LEAs now have these schools. In areas where all the schools are selective, approximately 75 per cent attend secondary modern schools.

FACT PANEL 2 (*continued*)

Middle schools. In some areas the pattern of state education goes as follows: first schools, for five- to nine-year-olds; middle schools, for nine- to twelve- or thirteen-year-olds; and secondary schools, for twelve- or thirteen-year-olds upwards. Middle schools, therefore, cater for what is usually the upper end of the primary age group and the lower end of the secondary age group. (Some children may be more ready to face secondary education at twelve or thirteen, rather than at eleven. Opinion is divided as to whether the middle schools have been successful. The problem seems to be that in some areas they have neither the staff nor the equipment to provide proper educational experiences for the secondary age children within them. Those middle schools, however, which have equipment and appropriate staff suitable for the first years of secondary education can produce very good results.)

VOLUNTARY-AIDED AND VOLUNTARY-CONTROLLED SCHOOLS

These schools may be primary, middle or secondary. Their buildings are usually owned by a church or some other foundation. In voluntary-aided schools the church governors are in the majority on the governing board and have to fund 15 per cent of capital costs. The LEA pays the rest. In voluntary-controlled schools, the church governors are not in the majority and the LEA bears all costs. Voluntary schools, therefore, have a measure of independence, which some parents may prefer.

TECHNICAL SCHOOLS AND CITY TECHNOLOGY COLLEGES (CTCs)

A few schools and colleges specialize in courses for particular skills and technology-related subjects for children between the ages of eleven and eighteen. Some take part in the Technical and Vocational Education Initiative (TVEI), funded by the Manpower Services Commission. There is usually an entrance test to these schools. The Secretary of State for Education and Science has promised that more than twenty City Technology Colleges (CTCs) are to be established after 1988. They will specialize in technological courses for children between eleven and eighteen and will not be run by LEAs. Full details may be obtained from the Department of Education and Science (address on page 112).

continued overleaf

FACT PANEL 2 (*continued*)

GRANT-MAINTAINED SCHOOLS

The 1988 Education Reform Act enables all secondary schools and certain larger primary schools to opt out of the control of their local education authority, if a majority of their governors and of the parents of registered pupils so wish. The schools will then be given a grant for each pupil by the government. This measure of independence may well enable the staff, governing body and headteacher to improve the standards of 'their' school. Certainly it will lead to a greater choice of schools.

If you dislike for some reason the educational policies of your local authority, you may wish to investigate those schools which have opted for grant maintained status in your area. A list will be available from 1990 from the DES (address on page 112).

Of course, you also have the right to choose to pay fees to educate your child outside the state educational system, at an independent secondary school (public school) or, at the junior stage, at a preparatory school. These schools, generally, have very good reputations.

In addition certain independent schools offer government-assisted places. If you cannot afford private school fees but feel your child is better suited to this type of education, you have the right to apply for an assisted place. In this case, if your application is accepted, the government pays some or all of the tuition fees (but not boarding fees if you do not choose a day

FACT PANEL 3

The independent schools

These schools are independently maintained and can be managed by a board of governors. They cater for both the primary and secondary age ranges and also for nursery classes for the three- to five-year-olds. They specialize in small classes and traditional methods of education and generally have an excellent reputation. All provide prospectuses free of charge and parents ought to ask the same kind of questions of headteachers of fee-paying schools as are recommended in this book for state-maintained schools.

Independent schools charge fees from roughly £600 a year for small day kindergartens, and from £2,750 to over £7,000 for the prestigious day and boarding schools. The vast majority of independent schools offer only day places.

Pre-preparatory schools, sometimes called kindergartens, usually accept pupils from ages three to seven and often have an associated preparatory school nearby.

Preparatory schools. These are junior schools which accept pupils from ages seven or eight to twelve or thirteen. Their job is to prepare children for the Common Entrance Examination for public schools or other independent secondary schools. The Common Entrance Examination is a nation-wide examination set by an independent board. The academic standard required to pass this examination varies from school to school.

Public schools (or senior independent schools as they like to be known nowadays) accept pupils at eleven, twelve or thirteen years of age. Admission is by interview and special test, or by the Common Entrance Examination. They have an excellent record of secondary examination results. Independent schools have 17 per cent of all sixth-formers and their pupils pass 25 per cent of all A-levels. They obtain about 50 per cent of all 'A' grades awarded. Most independent schools are single-sex schools, although more and more sixth forms are becoming co-educational.

About 6 per cent of children in the UK are educated at the 2500 independent schools. A very large proportion of these are 'first-timers', that is, their parents have not attended independent schools themselves. Their boarding facilities are particularly valued by parents who live or work overseas.

Assistance with all or part of the cost of fees is often given in the form of scholarships and bursaries. Some independent secondary schools offer government assisted places (APS) (see Fact Panel 9 on pages 75–6).

It is not necessary today to enter your child's name for a school soon after he or she is born. In fact, a few schools will have places up until a few months before the joining date. On the other hand, it is wise to book a place early – perhaps two or three years ahead, especially if there are not many independent schools in your area. To find out about independent schools, contact the Independent Schools Information Service (ISIS), which issues, entirely without obligation, lists of local independent schools. (see page 112 for the relevant addresses).

place), depending on your income. About 5,500 assisted places are available each year. You will find more information about the assisted places scheme and details of the parental contribution (if any) required towards tuition fees in Fact Panel 9. A list of those independent schools participating in the scheme is given on pages 85 to 91.

If your child has a physical or other disability, has social problems or other particular educational needs, special arrangements can be made. Your LEA must tell you what your rights are and how it cares for these children in both ordinary and special schools. Information about special arrangements at ordinary schools can be found at the end of this chapter. Information about special schools can be found in Fact Panel 7.

The right to information

Each school, primary or secondary, in the state sector (and each independent school taking part in the government assisted places scheme) must, by law, publish a prospectus giving details about its educational, social and religious attitudes. In addition, secondary schools are required to publish full details of all their examination results – GCE A-level and GCSE – for every subject. Schools must also make available details of their standard number (see Fact Panel 6). A copy of the prospectus will normally be posted to you on request, or you may collect a copy from the school.

Each LEA must provide information about the schools in its area and how to get in touch with them. It must also state its educational policies and welfare arrangements (see Fact Panel 5). This information must be made *easily* available to parents, free of charge, at least six weeks before they have to express a preference for a school. Normally your LEA will automatically send you the relevant documents and a transfer form in the autumn or spring term preceding the beginning of the school year in which your child transfers. If you have difficulty in getting the information you need, contact your LEA and insist on your rights, quoting the 1980 Education Act (see pages 92 and 93).

FACT PANEL 4

Information available from schools

The Education (School Information) Regulations, 1981, require that a school *must* provide you with the following information:

(1) The name, address and telephone number of the school and the names of the headteacher and chairman of the governors.

(2) The type of school.

(3) How parents can visit the school before making their choice.

(4) Particulars of the school curriculum: how it caters for different age groups; subject choices and how parents and pupils can make them; sex education; careers education, etc.

(5) Religious affiliations and details of religious education.

(6) Arrangements for pupils with special educational needs.

(7) The organization of the education of the school, particularly in respect of the teaching of children of different age and abilities together or in separate groups – either generally or in separate subjects.

(8) Policy concerning homework.

(9) Pastoral care arrangements.

(10) School discipline, including the policy on punishment, and how school rules are brought to the attention of parents and pupils.

(11) The main societies and activities available to pupils.

(12) School rules concerning dress and school uniform, including the cost of uniform.

(13) Information about the public examinations for which pupils are usually entered and the year when they take these examinations.

(14) Details of the GCSE examinations and GCE A-level examinations held in any year, giving (a) the number of the pupils in the appropriate year groups who, subject by subject, attained each grade in each such examination, and (b) the total number of pupils in each of the appropriate year groups.

FACT PANEL 5

Information available from your local education authority

The Education (School Information) Regulations, 1981, require that LEAs *must* provide you with the following information:

(1) The address and telephone number of the LEA offices.

(2) Arrangements for parents to obtain information about individual schools.

(3) The name, address and telephone number of each of its schools, together with the number and age range of its pupils.

(4) The type of school, i.e. primary or secondary, single-sex or mixed, comprehensive, grammar, secondary modern, etc.

(5) The religious affiliations of its schools.

(6) The general admission policy and standard number for each school.

(7) Arrangements for pupils to change schools at ages different from the normal admission age.

(8) Transport arrangements.

(9) Policy on welfare benefits such as free school meals and milk, or clothing allowances.

(10) General policy on entering pupils for public examinations.

(11) Arrangements for special educational needs.

The Education (No 2) Act of 1986 requires LEAs to provide each school governing body with an annual statement of recurrent expenditure at the school, and, as they consider appropriate, capital expenditure. This can be made available to parents in the governors' annual report (see Section 30 of the Act; Governors' annual report to parents, on page 94).

FACT PANEL 6

The standard number and school rolls (Education Reform Act 1988)

All schools have what is called a 'standard number' of pupils. This was the number on the roll in September 1979 or the number of its first full intake, if established after that date. From September 1989, all schools have to take pupils up to the limit of the standard number, or of the number on the roll in September 1988, *whichever is the higher*, if parents demand places.

The standard number will usually be higher than the roll for September 1988 as the school population has diminished dramatically during the intervening years. The standard number *may*, with the permission of the Secretary of State for Education and Science, have been altered if, for instance, portable classrooms in use in 1979 (or at a school's foundation year) have been taken away, or if the age group of the pupils has changed.

Until recently local education authorities have been able to ensure that less popular schools stay viable by placing an artificial limit on the pupil numbers at more popular schools. This meant that, although a school had accepted say 85 per cent of its standard number for which facilities were available, parents could be directed towards other schools.

AN IMPORTANT NEW RIGHT

Now the 1988 Education Reform Act has made this illegal. Children cannot be denied places at schools which are perfectly capable of admitting them.

It is well worthwhile enquiring, therefore, about the standard number of each school in which you are interested and comparing it to the number presently on roll. If the present number is lower than the standard number and you have been refused a place for your child, then you may have very good grounds for complaint. If there is a place in your child's age group and your child meets the other entry requirements of the school (you are unlikely, for instance, to get your son into an all-girls school!), then the school must accept him or her. The 1988 Education Act has therefore given parents a much wider scope for choice amongst their local schools.

continued overleaf

FACT PANEL 6 (*continued*)

If the number of pupils on roll at September 1988 was higher than the standard number then this figure, effectively, becomes the standard number. Some schools have had their standard number revised since 1970 (or their foundation) with the permission of the Secretary of State for Education and Science, usually because the school's accommodation has been altered.

From September 1989 all schools must accept pupils up to the standard number (or the number on the roll at September 1988, if that is higher) and utilise their premises and facilities to the full. If there is a place for a pupil of your child's age group and your child meets all the other entry requirements of the school, then the school must accept him or her.

A local education authority *must* inform you of the standard number for each school and the number on roll.

The right to appeal

Under the terms of the 1980 Education Act, if you are dissatisfied with the place allocated to your child at a particular school, you have the right to appeal. This applies to primary and secondary schools, both county and voluntary-aided or voluntary-controlled.

It also applies at any time after transfer when you might want your child to change school. It may be that you move, or that the educational policy of the school changes, or there may be medical reasons for wanting your child to transfer at a later stage (see Chapter Six). Your appeal is made to an appeal committee set up by the LEA in the case of a county school, or by the governors of a voluntary-aided or voluntary-controlled school. The appeal committee will consist of three, five or seven members, the smallest number being the most usual. There will be at least one member of the education authority and at least two other people with a knowledge of education in the area.

If you are dissatisfied with the educational arrangements made for your child, it is often possible to arrange an informal discussion with an education officer at which, hopefully, an agreement can be reached. If you fail to agree, the next step is to appeal.

The appeal procedure is quite straightforward. You will be advised of the date and time of the hearing. The hearing is private and informal. Sometimes several similar cases are dealt with at the same time, but you are entitled to an individual hearing if you want one. Some committees allow you to bring along a representative to speak for you. If you think this would be better for you, make your request to the appeals committee beforehand.

At the hearing you will be given the opportunity to express your reasons for preferring a particular school for your child, rather than the one allocated by the LEA, and of refuting, if necessary, the LEA's grounds for refusing your child admission. It is best to cite *positive* reasons for choosing your preferred school rather than the *negative* aspects of the one that you do not like. Both you and the LEA representative may be questioned by the committee. The committee will then consider your case, and will later advise you of their decision in writing. A successful appeal does not necessarily entitle your child to free transport to a more distant school.

Should the appeal committee's decision be unfavourable to you, you have two further rights of appeal: to the local Ombudsman and to the Secretary of State for Education and Science. However, it is very seldom that the decision of the appeal committee is reversed. On the other hand once you have won your case the LEA *cannot* overturn the decision and the LEA has no further right of appeal.

It is well worth making an appeal. Although it is difficult to assess accurately what proportion of appeals are successful, it appears that about 30 per cent is the national average.

Other rights

Free transport. You may be entitled to free transport if your child has to travel more than two miles to an infant school, or three miles to a primary or secondary school. So find out what your LEA policy is on this.

Special needs. There is a growing trend towards trying, if at all possible, to educate children with special needs in ordinary rather than in special schools. Each school has its individual and specialist ways of dealing with these educational needs. Ask the headteacher of the prospective school for specific information about these arrangements. Once your child is at the school, make sure that he or she is actually receiving the required attention.

LEAs vary enormously in how they provide for children with special needs, and in how rapidly they are trying to integrate such children into ordinary schools. If you do not think your own LEA is making appropriate provision, look at what other nearby LEAs are doing. Parents of children with special needs have the same right to go outside their own LEA as do other parents. If your child is accepted at a school outside your district or county, your own LEA will pay the other LEA, so long as it is within the provisions of the 1981 Education Act which specifically deals with special needs. Sometimes your LEA will even provide a place at a boarding school.

If you think your child might benefit from specialist education you also have the right to have your child's needs assessed by a specialist; the advice you receive is not binding. Your local education officer will provide more information about specialist education in your area. A list of special schools run by voluntary bodies can be obtained from the DES.

Remember you know more about your child than anyone else. So make sure you are satisfied with the arrangements made by your LEA. If you are happy for your child to go into an ordinary school, that's fine. But if you think a more protected environment would be better for your child, say so – and stick to your preference.

FACT PANEL 7

Special schools

Any child who has special educational needs, such as moderate or severe learning difficulties, physical or emotional disabilities, or sight or hearing impairment, is entitled by law to have those needs met. The LEA may make arrangements for the special needs of a child to be met at an ordinary school, provided that the placement would not affect adversely the education of other children and is compatible with the efficient use of resources.

On the other hand, the LEA may maintain special schools for children with specific disabilities. It may also place (and pay for) children at such schools, some of which may be boarding schools maintained by other LEAs or by voluntary bodies. There is a list of special schools in *The Education Year Book*, which will be in your public library.

CHAPTER TWO

Choosing a primary school

Schools, of course, differ in all kinds of ways. They range from the first class to the occasional very bad school. A poor school will provide an inadequate education for your child and you will want to avoid it. Children differ, too, in their educational and temperamental requirements, so do look carefully at all the schools within a reasonable distance before making a choice.

LEAs must provide a primary school place at the beginning of the term following your child's fifth birthday, at the latest. Many LEAs do better than this and admit children a little earlier. However, it may be that only a school further away can provide a place for your under-five-year old, and in this case you will have to weigh carefully the advantages of early admission with the disadvantages of increased travel and possible separation from neighbourhood friends. It is essential to talk directly to the headteacher of your preferred primary school about admission.

The procedure for choosing a school may conveniently be broken down into four stages:

☐ Reading the prospectus.

☐ Looking at the school from the outside.

☐ Visiting the school and speaking with the headteacher and staff.

☐ Making the choice of a school.

Reading the prospectus

Each school, as we have seen, is legally obliged to publish a detailed prospectus so, first of all, call or write for as many school prospectuses as you can. Do not forget the voluntary-aided and voluntary-controlled church schools or the schools outside your own LEA area, especially if you live near a county or borough boundary.

Then begin your assessment. Here are some useful pointers; they are summarized on page 27 as a check list on which you can enter the names of *your* schools.

(1) Check that the prospectuses give the information that the law requires.
(see Fact Panel 4 on page 19)

(2) How many pupils has the school?
(some parents prefer a smaller more 'homely' school, others the increased facilities that a large school may have.)

(3) Is there a list of staff?
(you may be interested in their qualifications, the ratio of men to women and the pupil/teacher ratio)

(4) Is there homework for older pupils?
(how much time must be spent on it?)

(5) Does the school have a church affiliation?
(whether it does or not, you may be interested in the policy on religious education).

(6) Does discipline appear to be taken seriously?
(are there school rules?)

(7) Are the names of governors mentioned?
(all schools must have at least two parent governors; are they listed so that you can contact them?)

(8) Does the school offer special curriculum subjects?
(such as computer work or a foreign language)

(9) Are competitive games mentioned?
(some schools are proud of their sports records, in others, games are virtually ignored)

(10) Are there any special facilities worthy of note?
(such as a swimming pool, school orchestra, etc.)

(11) Are school visits or clubs detailed?
(some schools mention educational trips and holidays and have after school clubs to encourage a variety of interests)

(12) Is there a school uniform?
(if so, what does it cost and where can it be purchased?)

(13) How far is the school from our house?
(help with travel costs can be available)

Finally, you might care to ask yourself if the prospectus is printed and produced well. A school that takes pride in its prospectus may well be one that takes liaison with parents seriously.

You may want to reject one or two schools at this stage, after reading their prospectuses; but do not rely on your reading alone. Visit the schools yourself to discover more about them.

Looking at the school from the outside

Do go to look at each school from the outside. It is best to do this at a lively time when the pupils are arriving in the morning, at break times, lunch time, or when school finishes in the afternoon.

How do the pupils behave? Are many late for school? Are there staff on duty? Are there any signs of bullying? Do pupils wear the uniform as set out in the brochure. You may care to talk to parents at the school gates and to ask other local people, such as shopkeepers, about the school. The neighbourhood grapevine can be wrong, but it can tell you things a prospectus does not.

CHECKLIST FOR PRIMARY SCHOOLS PROSPECTUSES					
Write in your local primary schools					
POINTS TO CONSIDER WHEN LOOKING AT PROSPECTUSES:	1	2	3	4	5
IS ALL THE LEGALLY REQUIRED INFORMATION GIVEN?					
IS THERE A LIST OF STAFF?					
HOW MANY PUPILS IN SCHOOL?					
ARE GAMES MENTIONED?					
RELIGIOUS EDUCATION/WORSHIP MENTIONED?					
SPECIAL FACILITIES/ACTIVITIES?					
IS THERE HOMEWORK FOR OLDER PUPILS?					
SCHOOL RULES GIVEN?					
SCHOOL UNIFORM COST?					
IS THERE A PARENTS ASSOCIATION?					
NAMES OF PARENTS GOVERNORS?					
HOW FAR IS SCHOOL FROM HOME?					
GOOD QUALITY PROSPECTUS?					
YOUR OWN POINTS: 1 2					

You may want to cross off more schools from your list after looking at them from the outside. But now you need to see inside the schools that are left.

Visiting the school

All good schools take pleasure in showing around prospective parents. However, do not expect to arrange a visit at the drop of a hat, as the staff are very busy indeed at certain times of the year. Some schools encourage new parents to visit in groups on a particular day; do go, but try to secure a personal interview later on a normal working day. A school which does not try to make this important first contact with parents easy and interesting may not take communications with parents very seriously.

If you have not visited a school since your own schooldays, it helps to plan well in advance. Make a list of specific questions that you want to ask. These can be based on what you have learned from the prospectus and what you feel your child needs from a school. Although you may not get a chance to ask all of them, preparation will give you confidence and help you to get more from your visit.

You may find the following points helpful; obviously you will not wish to ask about all of them. Use the handy check list on pages 31–2 to make notes on your local schools.

(1) Try to see as much of the school as you can.
   (Ask to be shown around. Check what you see against what you have learned from the prospectus. Check for instance to see how many would be in your child's class. The smaller the class, the more time the teacher can devote to each pupil. Shy pupils often progress more quickly in a small class.)

(2) How popular is the school?
   (Ask whether it has any spare places. If other schools in the neighbourhood are full, you may ask yourself why this one is not.)

(3) To which secondary schools do the pupils usually transfer?
   (You may have a particular one in mind for your child.)

(4) Do ask to meet the headteacher.
   (He or she is probably the single most important influence on a school. Notice whether the staff and pupils hold him or her in obvious respect. You will also want to know whether the head shares your own concerns about education.)

(5) Meet as many teachers as possible.
   (Most teachers are professional, hard-working people who will do their best for your child. Some schools, however, have been obliged to double up classes or even to close because of teachers' strikes during the past few years. You may care to ask if childrens' education has been interrupted in this way.)

(6) Note how classes are organized. Is there more than one age group in a class?
   (This is often called 'family grouping'. Some schools are set out in an open-plan way so that classes are never really separate. Some children and teachers find this stimulating; for others it is very distracting.)

(7) Does the school and its equipment look clean and cared for?
   (Even though the building and apparatus may be old, a good school will encourage its pupils to take care of things.)

(8) How much of each day is spent on reading, writing and number work?
(Are there special reading schemes? You may wish to ask how they operate. Many teachers are now returning to the phonic method of teaching reading – 'ter-a-per' spells 'tap' – rather than the 'look and say' method which requires a child to master a whole word at once.)

(9) What other subjects are on the curriculum?
(Some primary schools do useful work with computers; others use them as little more than toys. French is taught in some schools, not in others).

(10) What is the school's policy on religious education?
(You may wish to ask about sex education too.)

(11) Ask to see some classes in action.
(Remember, the teachers will not be able to spend long with you, so look for examples of pupils' writing and arithmetic as well as painting and modelling. Is the work corrected? No pupil will be motivated for long if his or her efforts are not marked by a teacher.)

(12) Is work available for you to see?
(Many subjects now are enhanced by 'project work', i.e. some extended investigation in a special area, for example the history of motor cars. You may wish to see some of this; it could be displayed on the walls or in folders or books. Look to see if it is marked or assessed.)

(13) Does the school test children's attainment in reading and writing and number work regularly and let parents know the results?
(Check to see if this happens and if not, ask why not. The 1988 Education Act will require this for all schools and testing will be phased in over the ensuing years. You will then have to be told your child's results in the test.)

(14) Can you see some sports?
(Many teachers believe that competition at school is healthy and you may want to ask about sports, teams and houses and whether there are ways for children to win points or marks for them.)

(15) Ask about teaching methods.
(There may be child-centred teaching which emphasizes the child's personal requirements rather than the understanding of traditional subjects. There may be traditional teaching methods involving what used to be called the 'three Rs' Reading, wRiting and aRithmetic.)

(16) Do the children appear to be friendly towards each other?
(It is very hard to judge a school's atmosphere in just one visit, but try to see if children and teachers appear to have a good relationship.)

(17) Do there appear to be any disruptive pupils?
(The presence of just a few disruptive children in a school can cause problems out of all proportion to their number. All schools have one or two difficult pupils. How are they dealt with so that they do not disturb the education of the majority? What punishments does the school use? What back-up from the LEA and the governors does the head receive if he or she wishes to suspend a pupil?)

(18) How does the school maintain contact with parents?
(Are there termly reports and parents' evenings? How quickly can you get an interview with a teacher if you are worried about something? Is there a time when you can reach a teacher by telephone?)

(19) Is there an active parents' association?
(This is often the sign of a popular school; ask members of the association known to you about the school.)

(20) Ask what arrangements are made for the supervision of children at lunch time.
(You may wish your child to stay to school lunch or bring sandwiches.)

(21) Enquire about transport to and from school.
(If the school is some way from your house, you will want to be sure that your child will not be too tired by the journey.)

Remember that you may not have time to ask about all the above. No school is perfect. All schools have problems, but a school which cares about relationships with parents will try to answer all your questions helpfully and honestly.

Making your final choice

When you have completed your visits, you will know quite a lot about the schools that you have not already ruled out. Don't forget that you can send your child to a school outside your neighbourhood, and even outside your local authority area if you can find a place.

Now you must make up your mind. Once you have chosen a school, apply at once in case places are very much in demand. Remember, you have the right to appeal if you are turned down for your first choice (see page 22).

Once your child has been accepted and has started, give the school every suport that you can. Join the parents' association and make a special effort to be at the parents' meeting when the governors present the annual report. Attend school events as often as possible and think of volunteering as a school governor or assisting in some other way. Above all, try to get to know the staff. Teachers are only human and are likely to respond well to your child if they find you co-operative and helpful.

CHECKLIST FOR PRIMARY SCHOOL VISITS					
Write in your local primary schools					
	1	**2**	**3**	**4**	**5**
YOU MAY WISH TO CHOOSE SOME OF THESE POINTS TO ASK ABOUT ON YOUR VISITS. IT IS OFTEN USEFUL TO FILL IN THE TABLE AS SOON AS YOU RETURN HOME.					

GENERAL INFORMATION
Did I get to see many of the classes?
 	
How many will be in my child's class?
 	
And in the rest of the classes?
 	
Are there spare places?
 	
To which secondary schools do pupils transfer:
 	
  1
 	
  2
 	
  3
 	
  4					

MEETING THE STAFF Did I meet the headteacher? Did I meet my child's future class teacher Has the school had to close recently, perhaps because of strike action?					

SEEING THE CLASSROOMS
How are classes arranged –
  open plan?
  separate classrooms?
 	
Does the school and its equipment look well cared for?
 	
More than one age group per class?					

CHECKLIST FOR PRIMARY SCHOOL VISITS
continued

	1	2	3	4	5
ASKING ABOUT THE CURRICULUM How much of each day spent					
on reading?					
on writing? on number work?					
on special subjects that I want to ask about?					
1					
2					
3					
Did I see some classes in action?					
Did they appear to be working purposefully?					
Did I see some reading, writing or arithmetic work?					
Was it neat and well presented?					
Did it appear to be marked?					
Are there currently regular tests of attainment in the essential subjects?					
Is sport taken seriously?					
Is there a 'house' or team system, with points to be won?					
ASKING ABOUT TEACHING Does the teacher say that his/her methods are 'child centred' or 'subject centred'?					
Would you say that the children are quiet and friendly?					
Are there any disruptive children? Ask!					
INFORMATION FOR PARENTS Are there parents' evenings?					
Are there termly reports?					
Is there a parents' association?					
Lunch time arrangements?					
Transport arrangements?					
YOUR OWN POINTS: 1					
2					
3					
4					

CHAPTER THREE

The General Certificate of Secondary Education

Examination standards have been in the news lately because the government has directed that a new examination must replace the General Certificate of Education (GCE) O-level and the Certificate of Secondary Education (CSE). This new scheme is the General Certificate of Secondary Education (GCSE) and all schools in England and Wales have adopted it in all subjects from the summer of 1988. Many schools in other countries, however, will continue with the British GCE system. School prospectuses have, therefore, shown the results of the GCSE from about autumn 1988. GCE A-level examinations will be unaffected by the change.

GCE O-levels have traditionally been taken by only the more able pupils. CSE examinations were aimed at a much wider range, but overlap with GCE O-levels, (a grade 1 pass at CSE being considered equal to a grade C pass at O-level). These have now been combined into one examination and there is a direct correspondence between the grades of the old system and that of the new. In fact, GCE O-level grades A, B and C (and CSE grade 1) have their equivalents in the new GCSE grades A, B, and C. The old CSE grades 2, 3, 4 and 5 are replaced by GCSE grades D, E, F, and G.

Comparison of O-level, GCSE and CSE							
O-LEVEL	A	B	C	D	E		
GCSE	A	B	C	D	E	F	G
CSE			1	2	3	4	5

A special feature of the new examination is that, although a pupil's grades in some subjects will mostly depend upon performance in the examination room, considerable weight in others is given to assessment (by the school's staff) of project and essay work done, over a period, in the classroom. This could help a child who is a nervous examinee. The proportion of course work contributing towards the final mark varies from

FACT PANEL 8

A guide to the examination system

Parents who are not familiar with the examination system in England, Wales and Northern Ireland, may find this brief account helpful. The Scottish system is different and information about it can be found on page 82.

General Certificate of Secondary Education (GCSE)

These examinations are designed for pupils of about sixteen years old, although they may be taken earlier or at any later stage of life. Grades A to C are intended for the more academic pupils – approximately the top 20 per cent of the ability range. Passes at these grades in at least five or six subjects are generally needed by young people who hope to continue with their studies by moving on to take GCE advanced level (A-level) courses and then to study for a degree or diploma at a university or polytechnic.

A similar number of good GCSE passes will be needed for young people hoping to go into occupations such as nursing or banking (see pages 113–64). So, if your child has ambitions like these (and the necessary ability and motivation), it is important to check that the school of your choice will give him or her a reasonable chance of passing these examinations in the appropriate subjects. Grades D to G are intended for a much wider range of ability. Pupils will be judged on work that they have completed throughout the course as well as by final examination. The proportion of coursework contributing towards the final mark varies from course to course. It will usually be 20 to 30 per cent but could be as much as 80 to 100 per cent.

General Certificate of Education (GCE), advanced level

These examinations are generally taken at seventeen or eighteen years of age, following two years of study after GCSE. They are graded by letters A to E. Students who do not pass a subject may be awarded N or U grades in that subject, or receive an outright fail (F).

If a pupil is hoping to go to university or polytechnic to obtain a degree, he or she will probably need at least two A-level passes (grades A to E). This is the basic minimum. Most courses will require more. For example, medicine, law and veterinary courses may ask for three grade As at

A-level; others may request combinations such as two Bs and a C. Generally polytechnic courses require somewhat lower grades than universities, although if a student makes a good impression at an interview, some universities may offer a place with minimum requirements.

General Certificate of Education, AS-level (advanced supplementary level)

This examination, which is offered in a growing number of subjects, is designed to follow a one year of study at A-level standard. Thus it is regarded as a half A-level and employers and institutions of higher education generally require two AS-levels in substitution for one A-level.

Obviously subjects cannot be studied in such depth as in two year courses and it is worthwhile checking to see whether, for instance, a university department, to which a pupil may be especially attracted, is willing to accept a combination of AS-levels. The examination is too new to allow much comment about standards or results as yet, but parents should compare AS-level results with those of other schools and consider the comparison as another helpful indicator.

General Certificate of Education, Scholarship level (GCE S-level)

These papers can be taken at the same time as A-levels, although they are of a higher standard. They are primarily for academic 'high-flyers' and help students who are applying for university places. Students who pass can be awarded a merit (grade 2) or, if they do very well, a distinction (grade 1).

Records of achievement

Because many important educational attainments are not reflected in examination results, the Government will introduce short summary documents called Records of Achievement to show what pupils have achieved and experienced during their time at school. It is hoped that these will provide a more rounded picture of pupils' abilities than can examination results alone, for the benefit of employers and institutions of further education. The Government is currently funding nine pilot schemes in England and Wales to gain experience before national guidelines are established.

course to course (and even from school to school). It will usually be 20 to 30 per cent, but could be as much as 80 to 100 per cent. It remains to be seen what value employers will place upon the GCSE courses which require only a minimum of formal examinations.

Parents will notice that study for the new exams in certain subjects involves more practical work and perhaps more visits outside the school, to museums or art galleries, for example.

New syllabuses have been devised and the Government has made available a considerable sum of money with which teachers have been trained in the details of the new scheme. Teachers now play a far greater part in the actual examining process, whereas the old GCE/CSE system confined them for the most part to *preparing* pupils for the examinations.

This book provides national benchmarks with which to compare the GCSE results of your local schools. The national benchmark is the national average number of passes per fifth-year pupil for all schools of a particular type. These benchmarks have been compiled from data based on previous GCE/CSE results because, of course, no GCSE statistics are available yet. The Government and the Secondary Examinations Council have made sure that the grades in the old and new systems are of equivalent standard, however, (as shown in the diagram on page 33) so the benchmarks transfer. After the new GCSE system has been operating for several years, further research *may* produce revised benchmarks; in the meantime, our tables are the *only* ones available for parents to use.

CHAPTER FOUR

Choosing a secondary school

Secondary schools can be of several types (see Fact Panels 2 and 3 on pages 14–17) and in Chapter Five we shall deal with the kind of things to look out for when you visit. There is one very important additional criterion which parents can use when they consider the prospectuses of their local secondary schools, however, for by law all schools have to provide details of their external examination results.

Our aim, therefore, in this chapter is to help you to make sense of information concerning examination results. We all know that there is more to education than examinations, but they *do* matter. Qualifications may be required for professional training or for other jobs, or for going to college or university. A comprehensive list of the qualifications needed for different careers is given on pages 113 to 164. Examinations are also important because they give an external and independent assessment of some aspects of the quality of teaching in a school.

All the schools and their examination results in this chapter are examples of the performance of real schools. Their names have, of course, been changed.

PARKWAY   RIVERSIDE   LIMETREE   CITYPLACE

Obtaining information about examination results

All schools, as we have said, are now legally required to give information about examination results to parents and they will usually post them to you. This information should include details of results for the General Certificate of Education Advanced level (GCE A-level) and the General Certificate of Secondary Education (GCSE). When obtaining examination results, parents should take into account the following points:

(1) Schools within the same area can differ widely in their examination successes. Therefore, you should collect the results from several schools. You can then compare these results and see which school might best suit your child's abilities and interests. If the schools send you details like those illustrated in Tables 1 and 2, you will be in a good position to choose a school.

(2) Make sure that the information which each school sends contains the details set out in this check-list:

   (a) The numbers obtaining each grade of pass in each subject: how many passes at grades A, B, C, D, E, F, G in each subject of the GCSE. Remember that grades A, B and C are those which are equivalent of the old O-level GCE passes.

   If the school has a sixth form, how many A, B, C, D, E and N grades in each subject at A-level.

   (b) The number of pupils in the fifth-year group and in the upper-sixth.

You will see that all this information is given in the example in Tables 1 and 2. Note that schools do not have to tell you how many pupils are given no grade at all but many schools do include these details in an open and honest way.

Alternatively, you may receive no information at all, or only very general information such as 'We achieved an 80 per cent pass rate in maths this year'. This is not good enough. Any school can obtain a high pass rate by entering only those pupils who are fairly sure to pass the examinations. Information of this kind can be very misleading. For example, if there are sixty pupils in the fifth year, and only two enter and pass GCSE maths, that is a 100 per cent pass rate, which sounds good. However, if thirty pupils entered and fifteen passed, the pass rate is only 50 per cent, but many more pupils have achieved a GCSE pass. So, in order to be able to compare schools, you need to make sure that each school sends you adequate information.

(3) Remember that all schools are required by law to give you this information (see page 19). If the schools that you approach fail to provide these details, insist on your rights. If any school refuses the information or provides limited details, you should write to the Chief Education Officer at your local county or town hall, your local councillor or the Secretary of State for Education and Science. You might also wonder why a school is keeping the information from you . . .

Two neighbouring schools

You can learn a great deal from the results for each school. A quick glance can show whether a school will give your child some chance of getting a reasonable GCSE or A-level pass in any particular subject. This is important because, although your son or daughter is probably only ten or eleven years old, he or she may have an aptitude or leaning towards a particular academic field or have some career in mind. You will want to make sure that the school you choose will give your child the best opportunity to prepare for it. Let us take some examples of real schools and see what they can show us (Tables 1 and 2, pages 40–1).

These are the actual results for two comprehensive schools in a poorer part of a large city. The schools are within walking distance of each other, and both are boys' schools. They have roughly the same sized fifth forms and almost identically sized upper-sixth forms. We will call them Parkway School and Riverside School. What can you learn from their results?

If your son is interested in modern languages, for example, you would notice that Parkway School has no A-levels at all and only four passes at GCSE grades A to C, but Riverside School has two A-level passes and fourteen GCSE passes at grades A to C.

In history, there is a striking difference. Parkway has twenty GCSE passes at grades A to C; Riverside has forty-three.

In general, you will see that the forty-nine pupils in the upper-sixth form at Riverside obtained twenty-one A-level passes, compared with the eight A-levels obtained by the forty-six pupils in the upper-sixth at Parkway. Thus, if you think your son might hope to stay on into the sixth form to continue his studies, Riverside School would seem the better place for him.

Comparing schools in your area

We have been able to compare these two schools because they are very similar in many ways. They are roughly the same size. They are both boys' comprehensive schools and they are in the same part of the city, taking pupils from the same sorts of backgrounds. But it is much more difficult to compare schools which are not so similar, even if they are all of the same type, for example, all comprehensive schools. It would not make sense to compare different types of schools such as a grammar school and a comprehensive school.

It is well known that the kind of neighbourhood in which a school is located is likely to affect the school's examination results. Schools in prosperous areas tend to get more and better examination results than those in average areas. These, in turn, do better than those in the poorer areas. You should, therefore, take this into account when looking at the results and when choosing a school for your child.

Here are a few easy steps which you can take to help you compare schools in your area with each other, and also with schools of similar types in similar areas in the rest of the country.

Step 1. Identify the type of school. Is each school a comprehensive, a maintained grammar school or a secondary modern school?

Step 2. Judge the kind of area in which the school is placed. Is it in a prosperous area? We have called this a Greenfields area in our tables. Is it in an average sort of area? We have called this a Middletown area. Is it in a poorer area? We call this an Innertown area.

TABLE 1

PARKWAY COMPREHENSIVE SCHOOL

PARKWAY STREET · INNERTOWN

Number of pupils in Upper Sixth: 46   Number of pupils in Fifth Form: 213

GCSE PASSES

GRADE	A	B	C	D	E	F	G
MATHEMATICS	1	5	21	10	21	16	28
ENGLISH LANGUAGE	0	1	13	10	26	33	15
ENGLISH LITERATURE	0	0	1	0	0	0	0
PHYSICS	1	2	5	6	2	16	11
CHEMISTRY	1	0	1	0	2	5	4
BIOLOGY	2	2	2	8	7	16	5
MODERN LANGUAGES	0	1	3	3	1	3	2
HISTORY	1	2	17	8	3	14	0
GEOGRAPHY	1	0	13	5	12	5	5

GCE A-LEVEL PASSES

GRADE	A	B	C	D	E	N	F
MATHEMATICS	0	0	0	1	2	5	5
ENGLISH	0	0	0	0	3	1	5
PHYSICS	0	0	0	0	0	2	5
CHEMISTRY	0	0	0	0	0	1	1
BIOLOGY	0	0	0	0	0	0	0
MODERN LANGUAGES	0	0	0	0	0	0	0
HISTORY	0	0	0	0	0	0	0
GEOGRAPHY	0	0	0	0	0	1	4
ECONOMICS	0	0	0	0	2	1	1

Other subjects, such as Art, Music, Sociology, will also be shown in your prospectus.

TABLE 2

Riverside Comprehensive School

Riverside Avenue · Innertown

Number of pupils in Upper Sixth: 49   Number of pupils in Fifth Form: 233

GCSE PASSES

GRADE	A	B	C	D	E	F	G
MATHEMATICS	3	4	14	1	14	29	21
ENGLISH LANGUAGE	2	8	16	27	21	33	14
ENGLISH LITERATURE	3	6	8	0	0	0	0
PHYSICS	1	5	5	8	10	19	11
CHEMISTRY	2	6	1	0	1	6	6
BIOLOGY	0	5	3	3	1	6	5
MODERN LANGUAGES	3	4	7	3	3	2	4
HISTORY	10	8	25	10	7	21	4
GEOGRAPHY	1	4	6	2	2	14	8

GCE A-LEVEL PASSES

GRADE	A	B	C	D	E	N	F
MATHEMATICS	1	0	2	1	1	2	3
ENGLISH	0	0	0	2	1	1	0
PHYSICS	0	1	0	1	1	1	4
CHEMISTRY	0	1	1	0	1	0	1
BIOLOGY	0	0	0	1	1	1	1
MODERN LANGUAGES	0	0	0	2	0	0	0
HISTORY	0	0	0	0	0	1	3
GEOGRAPHY	0	0	0	0	0	1	0
ECONOMICS	0	0	0	0	3	0	0

Other subjects, such as Art, Music, Sociology, will also be shown in your prospectus.

We can now begin to compare the schools' results with those of similar schools with similar backgrounds. We have already seen some results in Tables 1 and 2 (and more are shown in Tables 5 and 7). All the results on which the tables are based are from real schools; their names have, of course, been changed.

Schools are so different in size that, in order to make any useful comparison, you need to do one or two simple sums. You can then:

(*i*) compare each school's results with national standards for that kind of school, and

(*ii*) compare each school in your area with every other school of a similar kind.

Table 3 shows how we can put each of our schools in an appropriate category for its type and area. You can now fill in Table 4, putting each of your schools in the appropriate box. If you are uncertain which neighbourhood categories your schools are in, use the Middletown boxes.

It is quite likely that you may live in an area which has only

TABLE 3

CATEGORISING OUR SCHOOLS BY TYPE AND NEIGHBOURHOOD

Type of school	GREENFIELDS	MIDDLETOWN	INNERTOWN
COMPREHENSIVE	Use Table 9	Use Table 10 *Limetree*	Use Table 11 *Riverside* *Parkway* *Cityplace*
SECONDARY MODERN	Use Table 12	Use Table 13	Use Table 14
GRAMMAR	Use Table 15	Use Table 16	Use Table 17

TABLE 4

CATEGORISING YOUR SCHOOLS

Type of school	GREENFIELDS	MIDDLETOWN	INNERTOWN
COMPREHENSIVE	Use Table 9	Use Table 10	Use Table 11
SECONDARY MODERN	Use Table 12	Use Table 13	Use Table 14
GRAMMAR	Use Table 15	Use Table 16	Use Table 17

comprehensive schools. But do remember that even within one local authority, some schools will be in better-off areas and may well have greater successes with exam results. These schools may be within travelling distance, and so it is worth getting their results to see whether you want to consider sending your child to them.

Comparing your results with the national benchmarks

Having decided which boxes in Table 4 your schools are in, compare their results with the national benchmark for schools of that type and neighbourhood.

National benchmarks for the main important subjects are laid out in Tables 9 to 17 on pages 52–60. Spaces are provided so that you can fill in the results of your own schools. (Note that for the purpose of these comparisons, the national benchmark for English comprises English language and English literature added together). From this you can assess the strength of the English department of a particular school. You will then see if each of your schools is as good as the national figure, or better, or worse. Remember that GCSE grades A to C are considered the equivalent of the old GCE O-level passes.

Example 1: A Middletown comprehensive school – Limetree

Suppose you live in a suburb of a large city – not a very wealthy suburb, but not a particularly poor one either. Your nearest school is a comprehensive school. It would be like Limetree comprehensive and so we can take that school as an example. Let us look at Table 5.

GCSE (grades A to C)

Many careers require GCSE passes at grades A to C as do many institutions of higher education, such as polytechnics and universities. Let us, therefore, look first at GCSE passes in mathematics at grades A to C.

- (*i*) add up the number of GCSE passes in maths at grades A to C. These total 62.
- (*ii*) note the number of pupils in the fifth year: 206.
- (*iii*) divide the number of maths passes by the number of pupils in the fifth year: $62 \div 206 = 0.30$.
- (*iv*) find the national benchmark for GCSE maths A to C in Table 10, (Middletown Comprehensives): 0.22.
- (*v*) compare the figure of Limetree's results with the national benchmark:

SUBJECT	LIMETREE COMPREHENSIVE	NATIONAL BENCHMARK	ARE THE RESULTS BETTER OR WORSE?
maths	0.30	0.22	better

You will see that the results for Limetree are better than the national benchmark.

Another important subject is GCSE English at grades A to C:

- (*i*) add up the number of GCSE passes in English (language and literature together) at grades A to C: 111.
- (*ii*) note the number of pupils in the fifth year: 206.
- (*iii*) divide the number of English passes by the number of fifth-year pupils: $111 \div 206 = 0.54$.
- (*iv*) find the national benchmark for GCSE English (grades A to C) again in Table 10: 0.44.
- (*v*) compare the school's results with the national benchmark.

SUBJECT	LIMETREE COMPREHENSIVE	NATIONAL BENCHMARK	ARE THE RESULTS BETTER OR WORSE?
English	0.54	0.44	better

Limetree's results are, again, much better.

TABLE 5

Limetree Comprehensive School

Limetree Walk · Middletown

Number of pupils in Upper Sixth: 133   Number of pupils in Fifth Form: 206

GCSE PASSES

GRADE	A	B	C	D	E	F	G
MATHEMATICS	8	16	38	21	20	41	29
ENGLISH LANGUAGE	5	8	39	32	29	20	4
ENGLISH LITERATURE	10	18	31	0	0	0	0
PHYSICS	0	7	9	2	8	30	14
CHEMISTRY	0	5	9	3	7	11	9
BIOLOGY	1	11	25	11	10	31	11
MODERN LANGUAGES	4	14	37	27	19	40	11
HISTORY	8	5	18	9	10	15	14
GEOGRAPHY	0	5	12	10	16	21	22

GCE A-LEVEL PASSES

GRADE	A	B	C	D	E	N	F
MATHEMATICS	0	9	4	1	5	4	0
ENGLISH	0	2	6	6	3	0	0
PHYSICS	1	3	1	5	5	3	0
CHEMISTRY	0	2	2	2	3	6	0
BIOLOGY	2	6	3	5	1	0	0
MODERN LANGUAGES	0	3	1	4	5	4	0
HISTORY	3	5	0	2	0	3	0
GEOGRAPHY	0	0	0	2	0	0	0
ECONOMICS	0	1	4	4	2	1	0

Other subjects, such as Art, Music, Sociology, will also be shown in your prospectus.

GCSE (grades D to G)

Alternatively, your child may not be likely to obtain GCSE at grades A to C, and you may be more interested in the numbers of pupils passing at grades D to G. Let us look at, say, Limetree's biology passes at this level:

- (*i*) add up the number of GCSE passes in biology at grades D to G: 63.
- (*ii*) note the number of fifth-year pupils: 206.
- (*iii*) divide the number of biology passes by the number of fifth-year pupils: $63 \div 206 = 0.31$.
- (*iv*) find the national benchmark for GCSE biology (grades D to G) again in Table 10: 0.26.
- (*v*) compare the figure of Limetree's results with the national benchmark:

SUBJECT	LIMETREE COMPREHENSIVE	NATIONAL BENCHMARK	ARE THE RESULTS BETTER OR WORSE?
biology	0.31	0.26	better

Limetree's results are better.

If you do this simple calculation for all Limetree's results you find that by far the majority of examination results of Limetree comprehensive are better than the national average for comprehensive schools in similar Middletown areas. Table 6 shows how

TABLE 6

LIMETREE COMPREHENSIVE SCHOOL
GCSE RESULTS COMPARED WITH NATIONAL BENCHMARKS

SUBJECT	GRADES A-C			GRADES D-G		
	NATIONAL BENCH-MARK	LIMETREE SCHOOL	BETTER OR WORSE	NATIONAL BENCH-MARK	LIMETREE SCHOOL	BETTER OR WORSE
MATHEMATICS	0.22	0.30	☆	0.53	0.54	☆
ENGLISH: LANGUAGE & LITERATURE	0.44	0.54	☆	0.81	0.41	●
PHYSICS	0.10	0.08	●	0.20	0.26	☆
CHEMISTRY	0.09	0.07	●	0.14	0.15	☆
BIOLOGY	0.12	0.18	☆	0.26	0.31	☆
MODERN LANGUAGES	0.13	0.27	☆	0.23	0.47	☆
HISTORY	0.11	0.15	☆	0.22	0.23	☆
GEOGRAPHY	0.13	0.08	●	0.26	0.33	☆

☆ = better result than national benchmark   ● = worse result than national benchmark

Limetree's results compare with the benchmarks. It is worth-while comparing results in all the subjects that concern you.

Example 2: An Innertown comprehensive school – Cityplace

Only a few miles away from Limetree School, but within the same borough, there are other comprehensive schools. Some of them are in poorer areas, some in more wealthy neighbourhoods.

The next school we consider is another real school within an easy bus ride of Limetree School, so parents might want to consider it, too. This school is in an industrial belt around a large city, although part of its catchment area consists of a relatively wealthy, leafy suburb. But as most of the children come from inner-city backgrounds, we put it in the Innertown category.

GCSE (grades A to C)

Let us look at Table 7, and once again, let us consider math-ematics first.

- (*i*) add up the number of passes in maths at grades A to C: 4.
- (*ii*) note the number of pupils in the fifth year: 95.
- (*iii*) divide the number of maths passes by the number of pupils in the fifth year: $4 \div 95 = 0.04$.
- (*iv*) find the national benchmark for GCSE maths A to C in Table 11, (Comprehensives – Innertown): 0.21.
- (*v*) compare the school's results with the national benchmark:

SUBJECT	CITYPLACE COMPREHENSIVE	NATIONAL BENCHMARK	ARE THE RESULTS BETTER OR WORSE?
maths	0.04	0.21	worse

Cityplace's results are much worse. The national benchmark for comprehensive schools in other Innertown areas is five times greater than the results for Cityplace.

And now GCSE English (grades A to C):

- (*i*) add up the number of GCSE passes in English (language and literature together): 14.
- (*ii*) note the number of pupils in the fifth year: 95.
- (*iii*) divide the number of English passes by the number of pupils in the fifth year: $14 \div 95 = 0.15$.
- (*iv*) find the national benchmark for GCSE English (grades A to C), again in Table 11: 0.42.
- (*v*) compare the figure for Cityplace's results with the national benchmark:

SUBJECT	CITYPLACE COMPREHENSIVE	NATIONAL BENCHMARK	ARE THE RESULTS BETTER OR WORSE?
English	0.15	0.42	worse

TABLE 7

CITYPLACE COMPREHENSIVE SCHOOL

CITY STREET · INNERTOWN

Number of pupils in Upper Sixth: 7   Number of pupils in Fifth Form: 95

GCSE PASSES

GRADE	A	B	C	D	E	F	G
MATHEMATICS	0	0	4	4	8	20	21
ENGLISH LANGUAGE	0	0	9	12	20	15	7
ENGLISH LITERATURE	0	3	2	0	0	0	0
PHYSICS	0	0	1	1	2	7	4
CHEMISTRY	0	0	1	3	2	8	10
BIOLOGY	0	0	0	1	5	9	12
MODERN LANGUAGES	0	0	1	1	4	8	4
HISTORY	0	0	2	3	1	6	2
GEOGRAPHY	0	0	0	2	2	11	15

GCE A-LEVEL PASSES

GRADE	A	B	C	D	E	N	F
MATHEMATICS	0	0	1	1	0	0	0
ENGLISH	0	0	1	0	1	0	0
PHYSICS	0	0	0	0	0	0	0
CHEMISTRY	0	0	1	0	1	0	0
BIOLOGY	0	0	0	0	1	1	1
MODERN LANGUAGES	0	1	0	0	0	0	0
HISTORY	0	0	1	0	0	0	0
GEOGRAPHY	0	0	0	0	0	2	0
ECONOMICS	0	0	0	0	0	0	0

Other subjects, such as Art, Music, Sociology, will also be shown in your prospectus.

It is much worse. If you do similar sums for GCSE (grades A to C) in physics, chemistry, modern languages and history, you find that Cityplace's results are much worse than the national average for comprehensive schools in the more socially deprived areas. There are no GCSE (grades A to C) passes in either geography or in biology.

GCSE (grades D to G)

If you are more interested in passes at grades D to G here are examples and comparisons. Let us take a look at mathematics:

(*i*) add up the number of passes in maths at grades D to G: 53.

(*ii*) note the number of pupils in the fifth year: 95.

(*iii*) divide the number of maths passes by the number of fifth-year pupils: $53 \div 95 = 0.56$.

(*iv*) find the national benchmark for GCSE grades D to G in maths: 0.53.

(*v*) compare the school's results with the national benchmark:

SUBJECT	LIMETREE COMPREHENSIVE	NATIONAL BENCHMARK	ARE THE RESULTS BETTER OR WORSE?
maths	0.56	0.53	better

Cityplace's results are just better. Table 8 shows how Cityplace's results compare, subject by subject, with the national bench marks.

TABLE 8

CITYPLACE COMPREHENSIVE SCHOOL
GCSE RESULTS COMPARED WITH NATIONAL BENCHMARKS

SUBJECT	GRADES A-C			GRADES D-G		
	NATIONAL BENCH-MARK	CITYPLACE SCHOOL	BETTER OR WORSE	NATIONAL BENCH-MARK	CITYPLACE SCHOOL	BETTER OR WORSE
MATHEMATICS	0.21	0.04	●	0.53	0.56	☆
ENGLISH: LANGUAGE & LITERATURE	0.42	0.15	●	0.75	0.57	●
PHYSICS	0.10	0.01	●	0.19	0.15	●
CHEMISTRY	0.09	0.01	●	0.14	0.24	☆
BIOLOGY	0.10	0.00	●	0.25	0.28	☆
MODERN LANGUAGES	0.12	0.01	●	0.22	0.18	●
HISTORY	0.10	0.02	●	0.21	0.13	●
GEOGRAPHY	0.12	0.00	●	0.24	0.32	☆

☆ = better result than national benchmark   ● = worse result than national benchmark

Comments and conclusions: (1) Clearly, Cityplace Comprehensive School does not compare favourably with other comprehensive schools in Innertown areas in terms of its GCSE grades A to C passes. The picture for GCSE grades D to G is mixed: the results in some subjects are better than the national average, others are worse. (2) If your child hopes for high GCSE grades you would be well advised to look at other schools. Remember that Limetree Comprehensive School is only a short bus ride away! (3) If you are not particularly concerned about high grades for your child, but if he or she has particular interests, it would be important to look at the school's records in those subjects and compare them with the result of other schools in the same area.

Comparing advanced level results

We have not provided national benchmarks for GCE A-levels. We have concentrated on GCSE results because these are the exams which matter for sixteen-year-olds and which may open up numerous opportunities. A-levels are taken by far fewer pupils (only about 13 per cent of school-leavers obtain one or more A-level passes). Also, as the numbers are so much smaller, it is easier to judge a school's performance by simply looking at the figures. Moreover, the numbers of sixth-formers choosing a particular subject may change dramatically from year to year.

However, there are some points which you should bear in mind when considering the best place for your son or daughter to continue his or her studies at this level. It is particularly important to look at the number of passes and the quality of grades. If you turn back to the results for Limetree and Cityplace comprehensive schools (Tables 5 and 7 on pages 45 and 48), you will see that Limetree has many more passes and also many more higher grade passes (which might be needed to get into university or a professional training course.) Remember that these are real schools within easy reach of each other, and, that even if your child started at one school, he or she might be able to transfer to the other, especially for sixth-form studies.

A look at other types of schools

We have concentrated so far on comprehensive schools because the great majority of children now go to comprehensives. Less than 10 per cent of pupils in state schools now attend grammar and secondary modern schools, and only about 6 per cent of all pupils are in independent schools.

We now turn to these other kinds of schools. We will not discuss examples of examination results for these schools in detail. However we do give in Tables 12 to 17 the national benchmarks for secondary modern and grammar schools in each kind of neighbourhood. These figures in themselves tell many stories. For example, it is interesting to note how good the results are for the secondary modern schools, especially in English and maths, despite the fact that they do not cater for the most academic children in their neighbourhood.

We give no detailed information about independent schools. On average their examination results compare very well with the national GCSE benchmarks for any type of school and they tend to do outstandingly well at A-level.

Making use of the tables

Tables 6 and 8 show the full comparisons for Limetree and Cityplace comprehensives. As we have seen, the first and fourth columns are the national benchmarks for each subject. The figures in the second and fifth columns are based on the school's results and are found by dividing the number of passes by the number of fifth-year pupils, as already described. Thus, these tables give a ready reckoner for each school. You can calculate the results for the schools in your neighbourhood by inserting their results in the spaces provided in the appropriate tables on pages 52–60. Tables 9 to 11 are for comprehensive schools, Tables 12 to 14 for secondary modern schools, and Tables 15 to 17 are for grammar schools. This should give you a good idea of some of the strengths and weaknesses of the exam results of your local schools. In the next chapter we shall consider other things to look for when choosing a secondary school.

Examination statistics

The examination statistics in this book are based on the NCES Examination Results Research Project. For further information see:

Standards in English Schools, an analysis of the examination results of secondary schools in England, by John Marks, Caroline Cox and Maciej Pomian-Srzednicki.

Standards in English Schools: Second Report, an analysis of the examination results of secondary schools in England for 1982 and comparisons with 1981, by John Marks and Maciej Pomian-Srzednicki.

Parents of children living in London may be interested in:

Examination Performance of Secondary Schools in the Inner London Education Authority by John Marks, Caroline Cox and Maciej Pomian-Srzednicki.

The three reports are published by The Sherwood Press, 88 Tylney Road, London E7 0LY.

TABLE 9

NATIONAL BENCHMARKS

School type: **COMPREHENSIVE** Neighbourhood: **GREENFIELDS**										
	PASSES PER FIFTH-YEAR PUPIL									
	GRADES A–C					GRADES D–G				
	NATIONAL BENCHMARK	YOUR SCHOOL 1	YOUR SCHOOL 2	YOUR SCHOOL 3	YOUR SCHOOL 4	NATIONAL BENCHMARK	YOUR SCHOOL 1	YOUR SCHOOL 2	YOUR SCHOOL 3	YOUR SCHOOL 4
MATHEMATICS	0.29					0.54				
ENGLISH	0.55					0.77				
PHYSICS	0.13					0.20				
CHEMISTRY	0.11					0.15				
BIOLOGY	0.13					0.28				
MODERN LANGUAGES	0.18					0.26				
HISTORY	0.13					0.23				
GEOGRAPHY	0.15					0.30				

To compare a school's achievement in any subject with the national benchmark, divide the number of passes in that subject (either A-C or D-G) by the number of pupils in the fifth year. (See p. 44)

TABLE 10

NATIONAL BENCHMARKS

School type: **COMPREHENSIVE** Neighbourhood: **MIDDLETOWN**										
	PASSES PER FIFTH-YEAR PUPIL									
	GRADES A–C					GRADES D–G				
	NATIONAL BENCHMARK	YOUR SCHOOL 1	YOUR SCHOOL 2	YOUR SCHOOL 3	YOUR SCHOOL 4	NATIONAL BENCHMARK	YOUR SCHOOL 1	YOUR SCHOOL 2	YOUR SCHOOL 3	YOUR SCHOOL 4
MATHEMATICS	0.22					0.53				
ENGLISH	0.44					0.81				
PHYSICS	0.10					0.20				
CHEMISTRY	0.09					0.14				
BIOLOGY	0.12					0.26				
MODERN LANGUAGES	0.13					0.23				
HISTORY	0.11					0.22				
GEOGRAPHY	0.13					0.26				

To compare a school's achievement in any subject with the national benchmark, divide the number of passes in that subject (either A-C *or* D-G) by the number of pupils in the fifth year. (See p. 44)

TABLE 11

NATIONAL BENCHMARKS

| | PASSES PER FIFTH-YEAR PUPIL | | | | | | | | | |
| | GRADES A–C | | | | | GRADES D–G | | | | |
	NATIONAL BENCHMARK	YOUR SCHOOL 1	YOUR SCHOOL 2	YOUR SCHOOL 3	YOUR SCHOOL 4	NATIONAL BENCHMARK	YOUR SCHOOL 1	YOUR SCHOOL 2	YOUR SCHOOL 3	YOUR SCHOOL 4
School type: COMPREHENSIVE **Neighbourhood: INNERTOWN**										
MATHEMATICS	0.21					0.53				
ENGLISH	0.42					0.75				
PHYSICS	0.10					0.19				
CHEMISTRY	0.09					0.14				
BIOLOGY	0.10					0.25				
MODERN LANGUAGES	0.12					0.22				
HISTORY	0.10					0.21				
GEOGRAPHY	0.12					0.24				

To compare a school's achievement in any subject with the national benchmark, divide the number of passes in that subject (either A-C *or* D-G) by the number of pupils in the fifth year. (See p. 44)

TABLE 12

NATIONAL BENCHMARKS

School type: **SECONDARY MODERN** Neighbourhood: **GREENFIELDS**										
	PASSES PER FIFTH-YEAR PUPIL									
	GRADES A–C					GRADES D–G				
	NATIONAL BENCHMARK	YOUR SCHOOL 1	YOUR SCHOOL 2	YOUR SCHOOL 3	YOUR SCHOOL 4	NATIONAL BENCHMARK	YOUR SCHOOL 1	YOUR SCHOOL 2	YOUR SCHOOL 3	YOUR SCHOOL 4
MATHEMATICS	0.17					0.61				
ENGLISH	0.33					0.96				
PHYSICS	0.07					0.18				
CHEMISTRY	0.04					0.09				
BIOLOGY	0.09					0.30				
MODERN LANGUAGES	0.07					0.19				
HISTORY	0.10					0.28				
GEOGRAPHY	0.10					0.32				

To compare a school's achievement in any subject with the national benchmark, divide the number of passes in that subject (either A-C *or* D-G) by the number of pupils in the fifth year. (See p. 44)

TABLE 13

NATIONAL BENCHMARKS

School type: **SECONDARY MODERN** Neighbourhood: **MIDDLETOWN**										
	PASSES PER FIFTH-YEAR PUPIL									
	GRADES A–C					GRADES D–G				
	NATIONAL BENCHMARK	YOUR SCHOOL 1	YOUR SCHOOL 2	YOUR SCHOOL 3	YOUR SCHOOL 4	NATIONAL BENCHMARK	YOUR SCHOOL 1	YOUR SCHOOL 2	YOUR SCHOOL 3	YOUR SCHOOL 4
MATHEMATICS	0.18					0.61				
ENGLISH	0.36					1.01				
PHYSICS	0.07					0.21				
CHEMISTRY	0.04					0.12				
BIOLOGY	0.08					0.30				
MODERN LANGUAGES	0.04					0.16				
HISTORY	0.09					0.24				
GEOGRAPHY	0.10					0.29				

To compare a school's achievement in any subject with the national benchmark, divide the number of passes in that subject (either A-C *or* D-G) by the number of pupils in the fifth year. (See p. 44)

TABLE 14

NATIONAL BENCHMARKS

School type: **SECONDARY MODERN** Neighbourhood: **INNERTOWN**										
	PASSES PER FIFTH-YEAR PUPIL									
	GRADES A–C					GRADES D–G				
	NATIONAL BENCHMARK	YOUR SCHOOL 1	YOUR SCHOOL 2	YOUR SCHOOL 3	YOUR SCHOOL 4	NATIONAL BENCHMARK	YOUR SCHOOL 1	YOUR SCHOOL 2	YOUR SCHOOL 3	YOUR SCHOOL 4
MATHEMATICS	0.11					0.52				
ENGLISH	0.20					0.82				
PHYSICS	0.04					0.12				
CHEMISTRY	0.02					0.07				
BIOLOGY	0.05					0.20				
MODERN LANGUAGES	0.02					0.15				
HISTORY	0.06					0.20				
GEOGRAPHY	0.06					0.21				

To compare a school's achievement in any subject with the
national benchmark, divide the number of passes in that
subject (either A-C *or* D-G) by the number of pupils in the
fifth year. (See p. 44)

TABLE 15

NATIONAL BENCHMARKS

School type: **GRAMMAR** Neighbourhood: **GREENFIELDS**										
	PASSES PER FIFTH-YEAR PUPIL									
	GRADES A–C					GRADES D–G				
	NATIONAL BENCHMARK	YOUR SCHOOL 1	YOUR SCHOOL 2	YOUR SCHOOL 3	YOUR SCHOOL 4	NATIONAL BENCHMARK	YOUR SCHOOL 1	YOUR SCHOOL 2	YOUR SCHOOL 3	YOUR SCHOOL 4
MATHEMATICS	0.81					0.22				
ENGLISH	1.47					0.34				
PHYSICS	0.42					0.14				
CHEMISTRY	0.37					0.11				
BIOLOGY	0.47					0.14				
MODERN LANGUAGES	0.80					0.24				
HISTORY	0.36					0.12				
GEOGRAPHY	0.43					0.14				

To compare a school's achievement in any subject with the national benchmark, divide the number of passes in that subject (either A-C *or* D-G) by the number of pupils in the fifth year. (See p. 44)

TABLE 16

NATIONAL BENCHMARKS

| | PASSES PER FIFTH-YEAR PUPIL | | | | | | | | | |
| | GRADES A–C | | | | | GRADES D–G | | | | |
	NATIONAL BENCHMARK	YOUR SCHOOL 1	YOUR SCHOOL 2	YOUR SCHOOL 3	YOUR SCHOOL 4	NATIONAL BENCHMARK	YOUR SCHOOL 1	YOUR SCHOOL 2	YOUR SCHOOL 3	YOUR SCHOOL 4
MATHEMATICS	0.73					0.33				
ENGLISH	1.37					0.35				
PHYSICS	0.39					0.14				
CHEMISTRY	0.37					0.14				
BIOLOGY	0.43					0.17				
MODERN LANGUAGES	0.67					0.31				
HISTORY	0.37					0.13				
GEOGRAPHY	0.40					0.15				

School type: **GRAMMAR**
Neighbourhood: **MIDDLETOWN**

To compare a school's achievement in any subject with the national benchmark, divide the number of passes in that subject (either A-C *or* D-G) by the number of pupils in the fifth year. (See p. 44)

TABLE 17

NATIONAL BENCHMARKS

| School type: **GRAMMAR** | | | | | | | | | | |
| Neighbourhood: **INNERTOWN** | | | | | | | | | | |

| | PASSES PER FIFTH-YEAR PUPIL | | | | | | | | | |
| | GRADES A–C | | | | | GRADES D–G | | | | |
	NATIONAL BENCHMARK	YOUR SCHOOL 1	YOUR SCHOOL 2	YOUR SCHOOL 3	YOUR SCHOOL 4	NATIONAL BENCHMARK	YOUR SCHOOL 1	YOUR SCHOOL 2	YOUR SCHOOL 3	YOUR SCHOOL 4
MATHEMATICS	0.54					0.34				
ENGLISH	1.13					0.45				
PHYSICS	0.33					0.13				
CHEMISTRY	0.29					0.12				
BIOLOGY	0.29					0.18				
MODERN LANGUAGES	0.44					0.26				
HISTORY	0.28					0.13				
GEOGRAPHY	0.33					0.17				

To compare a school's achievement in any subject with the national benchmark, divide the number of passes in that subject (either A-C *or* D-G) by the number of pupils in the fifth year. (See p. 44)

CHAPTER FIVE

Choosing a secondary school: what else to look for

In Chapter Two we gave some suggestions on how to choose a primary school. Do look back at this, as some of that advice applies to secondary schools too; secondary schools do differ from primary schools in many ways, however. There is also a greater variety of secondary schools so, as well as looking at exam results, you must look for other clues and ask other questions. Once again, the various stages in making your choice are:

☐ Reading the prospectus and comparing exam results.

☐ Looking at the school from the outside.

☐ Visiting the school and speaking with the headteacher and staff.

☐ Making the final choice.

Reading the prospectus

In some parts of the country, there are different types of second-ary schools; grammar schools, secondary modern schools, technical schools and colleges, comprehensive schools exist side by side (see Fact Panel 2, pages 14–16). In other regions all the schools are comprehensives, but there may be, as we have seen, big differences between them.

It is worthwhile, therefore, sending for as many prospectuses as possible. Once again, do not forget the voluntary-aided and voluntary-controlled church schools and (especially if you live on the border of a county or borough) schools outside your LEA's area. Secondary age pupils can, of course, travel further than smaller children and so this means that you can cast your net rather further afield.

You can then begin your assessment of secondary school prospectuses and here are some useful pointers for your assistance. They are summarized as a check list on page 64 on which you can enter the names of your local schools for comparison purposes.

(1) Check that the prospectus gives the information required by law.
   (see Fact Panel 4 on page 19) and check especially that examination results are given in the correct form so that you can carry out the comparisons detailed in Chapter Four.

(2) Note the number of pupils in the school.
(too many and your child may feel lost, too few, say a comprehensive of under 500, and some subject choices may not be available.)

(3) Look at the different subjects which are available at GCSE and then check them again in the results lists.
(A mention of, say, electronics is fine, but what does this mean if no one passes GCSE electronics?)

(4) Check whether the school has a sixth form.
(If so, how many pupils stay on after the end of compulsory schooling at sixteen and what kind of courses do they take – for instance do the majority take A-level courses or do most take CPVE courses or further GCSE courses? If the school has no sixth form and its oldest pupils are about sixteen, your child will have to transfer to another school's sixth form, a sixth form college or a tertiary college, in order to take A-level or other courses. Sixth-form colleges and tertiary colleges (see page 80) give pupils more freedom at an early age, not quite as much as that enjoyed by university students. Some parents and pupils prefer this, others feel that the familiar environment of a school sixth form is better. Bear your preference in mind when you are choosing.)

(5) Does the prospectus tell you how many pupils go on to higher or further education in universities, polytechnics or other colleges?
(Pride in the success of such pupils can be a valuable indicator of standards in the school.)

(6) Does the prospectus tell you how many pupils get jobs when they leave?
(and perhaps how many go on to professional training such as in nursing, banking, accounting, estate agency.)

(7) Check the details given on career guidance.
(is there a careers teacher or advisory service, are there visits to local and national industries and good relations with local companies?)

(8) Look at the qualifications of the staff.
(For more advanced teaching, good specialist qualifications are vital (as well as good teaching ability, but you cannot tell that from the prospectus!). Mathematics, physics, chemistry and technology teachers are in short supply. Does the school have enough teachers qualified in these subjects?)

(9) Check what the prospectus says about religious education and worship if you feel that they are an important part of your child's education.
(They are legally required to be part of the curriculum at all schools, although you may, if you wish, withdraw your child. Sex education ought also to be mentioned.)

(10) Does the prospectus describe any special facilities?
(such as an extensive library, a technology centre, swimming pool, sports hall, language laboratory, etc.).

(11) Does the prospectus detail specialist activities?
(such as music, drama, holidays abroad, community service, associated youth organisations?)

(12) Is guidance on homework given?
(the time to be taken ought to be mentioned; homework is a very important factor in school achievement and should be taken seriously. It can increase the time for study by about 25 per cent. Grammar schools, independent schools and the academic streams of comprehensives may set two or more hours of homework per day for older pupils.)

(13) See what the prospectus says about school discipline.
(are school rules mentioned? These are essential and parents should eventually be provided with a copy).

(14) Note the details on school uniform.
(pride in a school uniform is often a sign of good discipline within the school. Some schools require older pupils to conform to a 'dress code' instead of insisting on uniform. The cost of items of uniform should be mentioned.)

(15) Note whether there is a parents' association.
(a good parents' association is usually the sign of a co-operative relationship between staff and parents and can be immensely helpful to a school.)

(16) Are the names of parent governors mentioned?
(at least two have to be elected by law in each school; you may find it useful to discuss the school with them.)

(17) How far is the school from home?
(some schools run buses and help with train passes and other travel costs may be available.)

Finally, once again, you might care to ask yourself whether the prospectus is printed and produced as well as those from other schools. *(A pride taken in this first communication with childrens' homes could mean that the school values contact with parents.)*

You may wish to reject some schools at this stage, after reading their prospectuses. Do not rely on the prospectuses alone, however. Visit the schools yourself to discover more about them.

Looking at the school from the outside

Just as with primary schools, do go and look at the secondary schools on your list from the outside. The impression gained from first-hand observation is valuable.

Is the school well kept and reasonably litter-free or are there

CHECKLIST FOR SECONDARY SCHOOLS PROSPECTUSES					
Write in your local secondary schools					
POINTS TO CONSIDER WHEN LOOKING AT PROSPECTUSES:	1	2	3	4	5
HAVE I CHECKED EXAM RESULTS? (as in chapter 4)					
IS ALL THE LEGALLY REQUIRED INFORMATION GIVEN?					
TYPE OF SCHOOL: COMPREHENSIVE; GRAMMAR; SEC. MOD; TECHNICAL; OTHER;					
HOW MANY PUPILS IN SCHOOL?					
HOW MANY GO ON TO HIGHER EDUCATION?					
JOB SUCCESS MENTIONED?					
CAREERS GUIDANCE;					
ENOUGH STAFF IN SHORTAGE SUBJECTS?					
RELIGIOUS EDUCATION/WORSHIP MENTIONED?					
SPECIAL FACILITIES?					
SPECIAL ACTIVITIES?					
HOW MUCH HOMEWORK?					
SCHOOL RULES GIVEN?					
SCHOOL UNIFORM COST?					
PARENTS' ASSOCIATION?					
NAMES OF PARENTS GOVERNORS?					
HOW FAR IS SCHOOL FROM HOME?					
GOOD QUALITY PROSPECTUS?					
YOUR OWN POINTS: 1 2					

graffiti all over the place? Do pupils seem to come and go as they please, or only at lunch time and before and after school? Does there seem to be activity going on well after the end of school? What do local people, especially shopkeepers, say about the school? Are there teachers visible in the playground when pupils are there? Does the school uniform as described in the prospectus appear to be worn? Do you see pupils wandering about the town, possibly truants? How about smoking or even solvent abuse?

First impressions can be wrong but you can learn quite a lot by looking from the outside. A visit inside, however, is still vitally important to help you make up your mind.

Visiting the school

Good schools consider parental visits to be very important and take pains to make sure that parents see all they want. Do give plenty of notice that you seek an appointment, however, as secondary schools have even busier days than primary schools and teachers will not thank you for wanting to come when examinations or medical inspections are in progress.

Once again, our advice is to plan your visit and your questions well in advance, as this gives you confidence if you have not been inside a school for a long time.

Join a party being shown around by all means, but insist on a personal interview as well, and on a normal working day. Don't forget to ask questions beforehand of friends or neighbours who may have children at the school. It is wise to ask to visit some classrooms and also such specialist areas as workshops and laboratories, if you are particularly interested in them.

You may find the following points helpful, obviously you will not be able to ask about them all; there is a handy check list on pages 69–70 on which you can mark the names of your local schools and your comments about them.

(1) How many will be in your child's class?
(The smaller the class, the more the teachers' time can be devoted to each pupil. On the other hand, a very popular school will be under pressure to add one or two extra to each class.)

(2) Ask if the school is oversubscribed (i.e. popular).
(Have pupils been admitted on appeal during the past few years?)

(3) Ask about any obvious gaps in the subjects offered or in the results supplied.
(You will have compared the school's examination results with those of other schools and with the national benchmarks (see Chapter Four). Look especially at essential subjects such as mathematics which are taken by every pupil.)

(4) Enquire about those particular subjects in which your child has an interest or special capability.
(If, for instance, you feel that your child has an interest in electronics, art or modern languages, you will probably want to hear about the school's arrangements for teaching these.)

(5) Ask how the teaching is organised.
(Is there 'mixed ability teaching', in which the slowest and the brightest are taught together in one class – some say to the detriment of both in some subjects – or are the classes divided by ability in different subjects ['setting'], or for all subjects ['streaming']? Which do you prefer?)

(6) Ask about the new GCSE examination (see Chapter Three, page 33).
(The new examination requires more work to be assessed by individual teachers and possibly more educational visits and projects. You may wish to enquire about the changes that the new examination has brought.)

(7) Ask to see some of the pupils' work.
(It is useful to see both exercise books, project work and also examples in the art room or workshop. Is it neat and well set out? Is it marked and corrected where necessary? Children are never motivated to do well if their work remains unmarked for long periods.)

(8) Enquire about the school's attitude towards sports.
(Some schools have excellent facilities for competitive sports, others do not take them seriously. Some children love sporting activities and gain a great deal from them; others may be better off occupied at community work, art or craft work or some other option, especially when they are older. Ask about your child's favourite games.)

(9) Do ask to meet the headteacher.
As in primary schools, the headteacher is by far the most important influence in a school. Do pupils see him or her regularly, at assemblies, for instance? Do staff and pupils appear to hold the head in obvious respect?)

(10) Ask about staff turnover.
(Continuity in teaching is very important when children are being prepared for examinations. About one in ten teachers moving on each year is fairly common; if there are many more than this, ask why. How long has the majority of the staff been at the school?)

(11) Has school been interrupted?
(Some schools in recent years have had to end lessons early, send children home or double up classes because of teachers' strikes. You may want to ask if education has been interrupted in this way.)

(12) Is the school clean, well decorated and tidy?
(It is very hard to keep a school's paintwork fresh and bright when hundreds of children are around, nevertheless, the school should be tidy and free of graffiti.)

(13) Does the equipment in classrooms, laboratories, the art room, gymnasium, music room, etc., appear well kept?
(You may see if the cloakrooms are clean and tidy; do pupils have lockers in which to keep books, or must they carry them around?)

(14) Follow up what the prospectus says about discipline.
(Discipline is even more important at the secondary stage, because even a very few disruptive pupils can cause very serious problems for other children. How are these problems dealt with so that the education of the majority is not disturbed? What punishments are available to the staff? Do the governors and the LEA support the headteacher if he wishes to expel or suspend a pupil. Have there been any violent incidents at the school? Is there a list of school rules?)

(15) Ask about truancy.
(Most schools have a few pupils who are hard to contain, but a few schools have truancy rates as high as 30 per cent for fourteen- and fifteen-year-olds. 'In-school truancy' can be a problem too at some large schools, especially those with split sites. Pupils can register in the morning and then simply hang about all day, rarely going to lessons. Ask about smoking and if there has been any problem with drug or solvent abuse.)

(16) Look at notice boards.
(They often tell you much about the valuable additional activities and clubs that the school has to offer. They may also indicate whether some teachers promote political views amongst their pupils, with, for example, posters about the Campaign for Nuclear Disarmament. You may or may not agree with CND, but schools must now deal with controversial political subjects only when they arise in the ordinary course of teaching and in an even-handed way.)

(17) Ask about pastoral care.
(Teenage children often have difficulties with their school work; indeed they may have other problems and need help and advice. Most good schools have a system of pastoral care which may assist them.)

(18) Enquire about sex education.
(School governors are now responsible for ensuring that sex education, if it is given, takes place in a moral framework and in a form which is acceptable to parents. If you feel that you require reassurance about this, ask the headteacher.)

(19) Follow up what the prospectus says about pupils' post-school careers.
(Ask about jobs taken up by recent leavers, and about how many go on to further studies at universities, polytechnics and colleges of higher and further education, etc., and how many stay on after sixteen, if this is possible.)

(20) How well informed are parents about their children's progress?
(Are there termly reports and parents' open evenings? How easy is it to make an appointment to see the headteacher or other staff? When is the best time to speak to staff by telephone? Do parents receive the results of tests and assessments? [From 1991 all secondary schools will begin to have targets in the separate subjects of a national curriculum; you will be told what your child will be expected to learn each year and then what he or she has actually achieved].)

(21) Ask about lunch and travel arrangements.
(You may wish your child to stay to school lunch or to bring sandwiches; you may want to know the cost of lunches and snacks and how the pupils are supervised at this time. Older children can, of course, travel longer distances to school and you may want to enquire about buses and trains and free and subsidised travel.)

Be polite, be persistent and do not be put off. You know your child bettter than anyone else. So make sure that the school is right for him or her. If you choose a bad school, or the wrong school now, it will cause you and your child much more trouble later on and you may have to change schools (see Chapter Six), so be firm in crossing any school off your list if you are disturbed about any important points after your visit or if the examination results compare badly with national benchmarks.

Making your final choice

Once you have looked at prospectuses, seen from the outside and finally visited some schools, you will have a good idea about which one you prefer. If, however, you are not satisfied with the schools in your district, look further afield, perhaps in another LEA. Children of secondary school age can travel further than primary school children so you can cast your net wider. Do remember that your LEA may not pay travel costs to other schools.

If you think you have found a school that is right for your child, stick to your choice. If you do not get your first choice of school, pester the Education Office. Insist on an informal meeting to discuss your child's schools with the Chief Education Officer or

CHECKLIST FOR SECONDARY SCHOOLS VISITS					
Write in your local secondary schools					
	1	**2**	**3**	**4**	**5**
YOU MAY WISH TO CHOOSE SOME OF THESE POINTS TO ASK ABOUT ON YOUR VISITS. IT IS OFTEN USEFUL TO FILL IN THE TABLE AS SOON AS YOU RETURN HOME.					
GENERAL INFORMATION How many in my child's class? Is school oversubscribed?					

ASKING ABOUT THE CURRICULUM
Any obvious gaps?
 	
Any special subjects in which my child is interested?
  1
  2
  3
 	
How is teaching organised?
  Mixed ability?
  Streaming?
  Setting
  Other?
Did I see evidence of pupils' trips and visits
Did I get to see pupils' work?
Was it neat and well set out?
Was it marked/corrected?
Is sport taken seriously?
Is there a house or team system?
Are my child's sports played?
  1
  2
  3					

MEETING THE STAFF Did I meet the headmaster? Is there much turnover of staff? Has there been interruption of school from, strike action?					

CHECKLIST FOR SECONDARY SCHOOLS VISITS *continued*	1	2	3	4	5
SEEING AROUND THE SCHOOL Is the school decorated and tidy?					
Is the equipment well kept?					
Do noticeboards indicate clubs and societies or political activities?					
ASKING ABOUT DISCIPLINE How are disruptive pupils dealt with?					
What punishments are available?					
Does the LEA support the head over suspension/expulsion					
Have there been any violent incidents?					
Can you see the school rules?					
How many pupils regularly truant?					
Any problem with drug/solvent abuse?					
ASKING ABOUT CARE What arrangements made for pastoral care?					
How about sex education?					
How about career guidance?					
INFORMATION FOR PARENTS Are there reports?					
Open evenings?					
Easy to see the staff?					
Regular assessments reported to home?					
Lunch time arrangements?					
Travel arrangements?					
YOUR OWN POINTS: 1 2 3 4					

Write in your local secondary schools

one of his assistants. Have a word with your local councillor, who is there to represent you.

If this does not work, *use your right to appeal* (see page 22). An indication that you are going to appeal is sometimes enough to change minds.

Once you have chosen a school for your child, support it as much as you can. In particular, do attend the parents' meeting at which the governors present the school's annual report. This is a good opportunity to ask questions and present any problems directly to the governors. Many parents feel more confident about presenting their queries and requests when they find themselves backed up by parents equally concerned about the same matters. Join in parents' association activities, attend school events and get to know the staff as much as possible. But if first impressions prove mistaken and you become dissatisfied with your child's progress, turn to Chapter Six.

How to change schools

Your first choice may turn out to be the wrong one. You may have been mistaken in your assessment of the school. Perhaps the school has changed, particularly if there has been a new headteacher – no other individual has more influence on a school. Perhaps your child's needs have changed. He or she may now have developed an interest in a subject not available at the school, or intends to embark on a career for which the school is unable to provide adequate preparation.

If your child wants to transfer later on, or if your first choice proves to be wrong, don't despair. You have the right to change schools and to choose another school for your child. This is not an action to be taken lightly, as the upheaval may set your child back socially or even academically in certain subjects for a while. But a change is possible at any time during the school year, although it may make most sense to change after the summer holidays or at the end of a school term.

If you do decide to change schools, you have all the same rights as you had when you made your first choice. So go back to Chapter One and remind yourself what they are. Then turn to Chapter Two for primary schools or to Chapters Four and Five for secondary schools, and start again. It should be easier the second time. Your experience with your first choice should help you to ask the right questions the second time around.

If you are convinced that your child is not prospering at school, your first important step is to talk things over with the headteacher and as many of the staff as you can meet. Then see if there is any improvement for a term or so. If you still feel that your child needs a different school, then start sending for prospectuses again.

One final word of encouragement. These days, people do move house frequently so most schools, even the most popular, have a few vacant places in their second and higher years. As your child is now less likely to be competing with others, your chances of getting the school you want may be much better than at your first attempt.

CHAPTER SEVEN

How your local education authority can help you

Since 1980, LEAs are required by law to give parents certain information about schools. This is a result of the 1980 Education Act. But that Act lays down only the minimum information to be given to parents. Any good LEA can, and should, do much more than this.

In a democratic society, parents are entitled to as much information as possible about such an important matter as choosing a school for their children. This is their right as citizens and as people who are paying, in rates and taxes, for the education service. In practice, many LEAs do much less than they should, and some do not even do what the law requires. This chapter suggests what a good LEA should do.

Good practice

Every LEA should let parents know their rights as set out in Chapter One. In particular, they should tell parents, clearly and concisely:

- ☐ How to choose one of the LEA's own schools (county schools).
- ☐ How to choose one of the voluntary-aided or voluntary-controlled schools within the LEA.
- ☐ How to choose one of the county, voluntary-aided or voluntary-controlled schools in another LEA.
- ☐ How to appeal if their child is not accepted at a particular school.
- ☐ What the parents' rights are to free transport to school for their child.
- ☐ How to apply for an assisted place at an independent school.
- ☐ What to do for a child with special needs.

The LEA should also send the prospectuses for about half a dozen local schools to every parent whose child is about to change schools or go to school for the first time. They should also make it easy for parents to obtain the prospectuses for any other school in the LEA. For a secondary school, the prospectus should clearly set out the GCE, A-level and GCSE examination results for the school as required by law.

This guide has concentrated on information for parents who are about to choose a school for their child. Information at such times is crucial since, without it, choice is blind. Information about schools is useful to parents at other times. It is also a valuable guide for school governors, local councillors and the public.

Ideal practice

Ideally, LEAs should also give all parents of pupils at the school and school governors of each school, every year, the same information about the school as is given to prospective parents. This enables parents and governors to check standards from year to year and to identify strengths and weaknesses in individual subjects. They should also give local councillors the same information, every year, for all schools in the LEA and make it easily available to individual members of the public. Teachers and educational advisors should also receive the information each year as a matter of routine. The provision of all this information by every LEA would do much to stimulate genuine and well-informed public debate about standards in education in all parts of the country.

Each LEA should make every effort to supply additional pupil places above the 'standard numbers' (see Fact Panel 6, page 21) at successful schools. Less popular schools must be improved or face dwindling rolls.

There is no reason why your LEA should not do everything set out as good practice in this chapter. Yet many do not. So if your LEA is secretive, demand, politely and persistently, the information that you need.

Always remember that a good education is one of the most important things you can give your child. It is worth taking the trouble to find it.

FACT PANEL 9

Assisted places scheme

Certain independent schools participate in the Government assisted places scheme, instituted in 1981. Over 5,500 assisted places are made available each year in England and Wales (and a further 500 places in Scotland) for academically able children whose parents cannot afford all or some of the tuition fees.

Assisted places are normally available for pupils entering independent schools at eleven, thirteen or directly into the sixth form. Children of other ages *may* be admitted to the scheme, but only if they are able to be admitted to a class containing other pupils who already have held assisted places at the school since the previous school year.

It does not matter what kind of school your child attends before he or she takes up an assisted place, but the majority of places offered by a school must be given to children from state schools.

The scheme is administered by the Department of Education and Science, not your local education authority. To be eligible a child must have been ordinarily resident in the UK, Channel Isles or the Isle of Man for two years preceding the 1st of January of the year in which the place is to be taken up (there are special rules if your child has been with you whilst you were working overseas).

Application for a place is made directly to the school concerned (see pages 85 to 91) for list of participating schools). Successful applications are determined by interview and examination at the school, generally on the basis of academic ability or special talent. Because the number of places is limited (about 27,000 in England and Wales plus 2600 in Scotland*) competition is very keen. There are no participating schools in Northern Ireland. Parents may apply, however, for places at schools in England, Scotland or Wales; presumably they make arrangement for their child to board or stay with guardians.

Assistance with tuition fees is available on a sliding scale depending on your family income. Assisted places are normally meant for day pupils and no assistance is available for boarding fees. If, however, you wish your child to

continued overleaf

*35,000 places will be available by the mid-1990s.

FACT PANEL 9 (*continued*)

board, some schools may themselves be able to offer bursaries for boarding fees.

Some families may also be eligible for help with school meals (not after 1989) and uniform and travel costs.

For the schools years 1988/9, you do not have to pay anything if your family income for the tax year 1987/8 was £7258 or less. You do not have to include child benefit, mobility allowance, scholarships or student awards in this income, but parents are obliged to provide documentary evidence of their income (e.g. Form P60) each year that their child participates in the scheme.

If your family income exceeds £7258, the following table is a guide to what you are expected to pay in fees during the school year 1988/9. The figures are adjusted each year to take account of inflation and are available from the DES (or the Welsh and Scottish Education Departments) each spring. Do check to find out the latest figures.

| Relevant income 1987–88 tax year (after allowances for dependants) | Parents' contribution of fees: 1988–89 school year | |
	One assisted place holder	For each of two assisted place holders
£	£	£
7259	15	9
8000	90	66
9000	228	171
10000	402	303
11000	612	459
12000	837	627
13000	1077	807
14000	1317	987
15000	1647	1233
16000	1977	1482
17000	2307*	1728

*The maximum relevant income at which pupils will be eligible for assistance will vary in relation to schools' fees. In many schools the fees will not be as high as this and where this is so parents at this level of income will be ineligible for assistance.

There is more about the assisted places scheme in Scotland and Northern Ireland on pages 83 and 84, and list of all participating schools on pages 85–91. Information is also obtainable from the DES, and the Welsh Office (see addresses on p.112)

Conclusion

Choosing a school is not an easy task, and in your area the number of schools available may be limited even if you are close to an education authority boundary with the wider variety that this can bring.

It is well worth while taking the trouble to exercise your choice wisely. The school which your son or daughter finally attends will respect you for asking careful questions about its aims and its record, and will realize that you take your child's education very seriously.

Once your child is settled at a school, do go along to parents' evenings as often as possible. Join the parents' association and get to know the staff, governors and headteacher. Ask to speak to teachers regularly and attend school events as frequently as you can. The better you and the staff know each other, the less likelihood there is of your child's education going wrong. If you have the time, do volunteer to play an active part in the parents' association or to become an elected parent governor. Try to give the school every possible support.

Your children's schooldays, and the opportunities that they bring, come only once. It is worth making sure that they are spent in a school in which you have confidence.

A

compendium

of helpful

information

SECTION ONE: Choosing at sixteen

SECTION TWO: Information for parents living in Scotland

SECTION THREE: Information for parents living in Northern
                    Ireland

SECTION FOUR: The assisted places scheme: schools
                    participating in England, Wales and Scotland

SECTION FIVE: Relevant sections from the Education Act
                    1980, the Education (No 2) Act 1986 and the
                    Education Reform Act 1988

SECTION SIX: Addresses of local education authorities

SECTION SEVEN: Some useful addresses

SECTION EIGHT: A guide to career requirements:

                        COMPUTATIONAL/MATHEMATICAL
                        CREATIVE
                        GENERAL SERVICE
                        LITERARY
                        OUTDOOR
                        PUBLIC SERVICE
                        SCIENTIFIC

Choosing at sixteen

When your son or daughter reaches the official school-leaving age at sixteen, there are many possibilities for continuing education in the following two or more years. These include:

(1) Staying on at the school at which GCSEs have been taken, if it has a sixth form. Further GCSEs, GCE A-levels, the CPVE (Certificate of Prevocational Education) and other qualifications can be taken.

(2) Transferring to the sixth form of another maintained school, either inside or outside your local authority area.

(3) Transferring to a sixth form college. This is a school for those aged sixteen-plus which offers courses similar to those of a sixth form, but in a more student-like atmosphere. Some LEAs require a minimum number of GCSEs for entry to sixth form colleges, others have open access.

(4) Transferring to a college of further education (FE), offering to sixteen- to nineteen-year-olds a wide range of courses, usually vocationally directed.

(5) Transferring to a tertiary college, a large institution which combines the functions of a sixth form and an FE college.

(6) Applying for a government assisted place at sixth-form level in an independent school (see Fact Panel on page 75). A considerable number of places are reserved for entry at this stage. Good passes in GCSE will be required.

(7) Attending an independent school or tutorial college as a feepayer. (See pages 16–17).

(8) Transferring to the sixth form of a City Technology College (CTC), or grant-maintained school (see pages 15–16).

(9) Seeking a place on a Youth Training Scheme (YTS) or Manpower Services Commission (MSC) programme.

(10) Obtaining a job which offers the possibility of part-time day-release study.

(11) Studying at a part-time evening course.

LEAs in your area will provide details about sixth form colleges, colleges of further education, tertiary colleges and part-time evening classes. Details about the Youth Training Scheme are available from your local careers office. The Manpower Services

Commission programmes can be obtained from your local Job Centre. Addresses of the local careers office and of the Job Centre will be listed in the telephone directory.

It would require another book to describe the variety of courses available for the sixteen to nineteen age group, but because young people are very much more able to look after themselves at sixteen and to travel further than when they are younger, it is worth sending for brochures from a wider area and from several LEAs.

Entrance to universities, polytechnics and other institutions of higher education usually require good passes in a number of A-level GCEs and details can be obtained from the Universities Central Council on Admissions (UCCA) and the Polytechnic Central Admissions System (PCAS); the addresses are given on page 112. Alternatively the individual institutions themselves will provide detailed information.

Information for parents living in Scotland

The principles involved in choosing a school are the same throughout the United Kingdom. However, in Scotland the examination system is somewhat different and the benchmarks found earlier in this book cannot be used.

For example, whilst in England, Wales and Northern Ireland, A-levels are usually taken at eighteen, Scottish pupils have been taking the Higher Grade of the Scottish Certificate of Education, generally known as 'Highers', at the age of seventeen. Two recent influential reports, however, called the Munn and Dunning reports, have led to major changes in that Ordinary Grade of the Scottish Certificate of Education (SCE) which is taken earlier.

Until recently the SCE had an Ordinary Grade in most subjects, but this was phased out in mathematics, social and vocational skills, science and English in 1986 and replaced by a Standard Grade. In 1989, art and design, computing studies, contemporary social studies, craft and design, French, home economics and Latin will also be examined at Standard Grade and the rest of the school subjects will follow during the subsequent five years. The Standard Grade course is designed for all young people in the third and fourth years of secondary education in Scotland. After the fourth year, suitably qualified pupils take subject courses leading to Higher Grade (H-grade).

The Ordinary Grade was thought to be not sufficiently challenging for the brightest pupils and to leave many others with a sense of failure. The new Standard Grade has three levels and seven grades:

Grades 1 and 2:	Credit level
Grades 3 and 4:	General level
Grades 5 and 6:	Foundation level
Grade 7:	merely denotes that the pupil has finished the course

A varying proportion of the mark awarded will be based upon teachers' judgements of the work done by the pupils over the whole course. Thus pupils who do well in class, but whose written examinations are not as good as expected, will still get recognition for what they have achieved.

Until 1991 there will still be Ordinary Grade examinations available, as we have seen, in many subjects. Their marks will be reported on grades 1 to 5 of the Standard scale above, instead of the old A, B, C, etc., grades.

☐ The new Standard Grade 1 broadly equates to the old Ordinary Grade A.

☐ The new Standard Grade 2 broadly equates to the upper marks in the old Grade B.

☐ The new Standard Grade 3 is broadly equivalent to the lower part of Ordinary Grade B plus Grade C.

Many employers and institutions of higher education are likely, therefore to regard only Standard Grades 1, 2, and 3 as being suitable passes for entrance purposes.

Most pupils will sit papers which will cover two levels for each subject, covering four grades. So a bright pupil would probably sit papers for the Credit and General levels, whilst those with less ability would sit for General and Foundation levels. The Foundation level is for those who would have been unlikely to obtain any passes at the Ordinary Grade SCE.

'Highers' will continue, however, to be the target for the most able pupils. Those who obtain an overall award of Standard Grade 1 or 2 will normally take the Higher Grade examination in their fifth year, after just one years' further study. Other pupils will probably require two years' study in order to sit the Higher Grade examinations.

Not all schools, however, will be able to offer two-year Higher Grade courses. This may be something you may wish to ask about when you are choosing a school. Some changes in the Higher Grade examinations may have to be made as a result of the new Standard Grade courses. Parents who are interested in these changes can obtain further information from the Scottish Education Department (address page 112). There is a concise and informative brochure available from the same source and called *Choosing a School, a Guide to Parents*.

Assisted places scheme

In Scotland about 2,600 pupils take part in the assisted places scheme and there are about 500 new places available each year. A list of Scottish independent schools taking part in the scheme can be found on pages 90–1. Full details can be found in Fact Panel 9 (page 75); the scale of parental contributions required towards fees is standard throughout the United Kingdom and can be found on page 76.

Careers guide

Parents in Scotland can make good use of the guide to careers on pages 113 to 165, but should remember that some careers may require different grades from those specified elsewhere in the United Kingdom.

Information for parents living in Northern Ireland

In Northern Ireland there are more selective schools than in most parts of England and Wales. In other words, there are relatively more secondary modern and grammar schools still in existence: in fact, a similar situation to that in England and Wales before the great shift to comprehensive education. Consequently, in Ulster, you will need to make appropriate comparisons for the schools you are considering, taking care to compare like with like. You will find the tables giving benchmarks for comparison with other grammar and secondary modern schools in different kinds of areas. But do remember that, although grammar schools must be expected to get better results than secondary modern schools, national research has shown that many secondary modern schools do as well. In some parts of England and Wales they provide their pupils with better examination results than their counterparts in comprehensives. Parents in Ulster might be cheered to know that in recent years overall examination performance (in terms of proportions of each age group leaving with various numbers of GCE O-level, CSE, and GCE A-level passes) has improved in Northern Ireland, relative to England and Wales.

Assisted places

In Northern Ireland there are presently no independent schools participating in the assisted places scheme. Parents, however, may apply for places at schools in England, Scotland and Wales. Tuition fees only are payable under the scheme, however and not the cost of boarding (see Fact Panel 9, page 75).

The assisted places scheme: schools participating in England, Wales and Scotland

B = boys G = girls M = mixed *b* = boarding places available
Figures in brackets show the number of sixth form places available. In certain schools, boarding places are only available for sixth-form pupils.

	Boys/ girls/ mixed	Normal age of entry	Annual number of places
England			
NORTH-EAST			
Royal Grammar School, Newcastle upon Tyne	B	11, 13	55(5)
Dame Allan's Boys' School, Newcastle upon Tyne	B	11, 12, 13	27(5)
Dame Allan's Girls' School, Newcastle upon Tyne	G	11	20(5)
Central Newcastle High School, Newcastle upon Tyne	G	11	18(5)
La Sagesse Convent RC School, Newcastle upon Tyne	G	11	25(5)
NORTH-WEST **Cumbria and Lancashire**			
St Bees School	M*b*	11, 13	12(5)
Casterton School, Kirkby Lonsdale	G*b*	11, 12, 13	8(4)
Sedbergh School	B*b*	11	5(5)
Stonyhurst RC College, Whalley, Blackburn	B*b*	11, 13	5(2)
Queen Elizabeth's Grammar School, Blackburn	B	11, 12, 13	40(5M*b*)
Rossall School, Fleetwood	M*b*	13	6(4)
Arnold School, Blackpool	M*b*	11	10(5)
King Edward VII School Lytham	B	11, 13	34(5)
Queen Mary School, Lytham	G	13	38(5)
Kirkham Grammar School	M	11	10(5)
MERSEYSIDE			
St Edward's RC College, Sandfield Park, Liverpool	B	11	55(5)
Liverpool College, Mossley Hill	B	11	25(5M*b*)
Belvedere School, Prince's Park, Liverpool	G	11	25(5)
St Mary's RC College, Great Crosby	B	11, 13	40(5M*b*)
Merchant Taylors' School, Crosby	B	11, 13	33(5)
Merchant Taylors' Girls School, Crosby	G	11	28(5)
Birkenhead School	B	11, 13	40(5)
St Anselm's RC College, Birkenhead	B	11	30(5)
Birkenhead High School	G	11	40(5)
Upton Hall Convent RC School, Wirral	G	11, 12, 13	30(5)
GREATER MANCHESTER AND CHESHIRE			
Bolton School (Boys' Division)	B	11	38(5)
Bolton School (Girls' Division)	G	11	38(5)

	Boys/ girls/ mixed	Normal age of entry	Annual number of places
Bury Grammar School (Boys)	B	11	30(5)
Bury Grammar School (Girls)	G	11	35(5)
Hulme Grammar School (Boys), Oldham	B	11	30(5)
Hulme Grammar School (Girls), Oldham	G	11	30(5)
Manchester Grammar School	B	11	40(5)
William Hulme's Grammar School, Manchester	B	11	30(5)
St Bede's RC College, Alexandra Pk, Manchester	B	11	30(5M*b*)
Manchester High School, Grangethorpe Rd, Manchester	G	11	25(5)
Withington Girls' School, Fallowfield, Manchester	G	11	15(3)
Stockport Grammar School	M	11	40(5)
Cheadle Hulme School, Cheadle	M*b*	11	20(5)
St Ambrose RC College, Hale Barns, Altrincham	B	11	15(5)
Loreto Convent RC Grammar School, Altrincham	G	11, 12, 13	13(5)
The King's School, Macclesfield	B	11, 13	30(5)
The King's School, Chester	B	11	16(5)
The Queen's School, Chester	G	11	12(5)

YORKSHIRE AND HUMBERSIDE

Harrogate College	G*b*	11	5(2)
St Peter's School, York	B	11, 13	25(5M*b*)
Pocklington School, Nr York	B*b*	11, 13	20(3)
Hymers College, Hull	B	11, 13	28(5M*b*)
Batley Grammar School, Carlinghow Hill, Batley	B	11, 12, 13	40(5)
Bradford Grammar School, Keighley Road, Bradford	B	11, 13	30
Bradford Girls' Grammar School, Squire Lane, Bradford	G	11, 12, 13	10
Woodhouse Grove School, Apperley Bridge, Bradford	B	11, 13	23(5M*b*)
Leeds Grammar School, Moorland Road, Leeds	B	11, 12, 13	35(5)
Leeds Girls' High School, Headingley Lane, Leeds	G	11, 12, 13	20(5)
Queen Elizabeth Grammar School, Wakefield	B*b*	11, 12	25(5)
Wakefield High School	G	11, 13	22(5)
Sheffield High School, Rutland Park, Sheffield	G	11	16(5M)

EAST MIDLANDS

Mount St Mary's RC College, Spinkhill, Derbyshire	M*b*	11, 13	10(5)
Repton School, Derby	B	11, 13	6(5M*b*)
Trent College, Long Eaton	B	11, 12, 13	20(5M*b*)
Nottingham High School	B	11	20(5)
Nottingham Girls' High School, Arboretum St., Nottingham	G	11	30(5)
Loughborough Grammar School	B*b*	11, 13	18(5)
Loughborough High School	G*b*	11, 13	14(5)
Ratcliffe RC College, Syston, Nr Leicester	B	11, 13	12(2M*b*)
Stamford School	B*b*	11, 12, 13	20(5)
Stamford High School	G*b*	11	15(5)
Wellingborough School	M*b*	11, 13	10(5)
Northampton High School, Derngate, Northampton	G	11, 13	35(5)
Bedford School, Burnaby Road, Bedford	B*b*	11, 13	20(3)
Bedford High School, Bromham Road, Bedford	G*b*	11, 13	20(3)
Bedford Modern School, Manton Lane, Bedford	B*b*	11, 13	20(3)
Dame Alice Harpur School, Cardington Rd, Bedford	G	11, 13	20(3)

	Boys/girls/mixed	Normal age of entry	Annual number of places
WEST MIDLANDS			
Warwick School	B*b*	11, 12, 13	25(5)
King's High School, Warwick	G	11	30(5)
Coventry School	M	11	35(5)
King Edward's School, Birmingham	B	11, 13	42(5)
King Edward VI High School, Birmingham	G	11	25(5)
Wolverhampton Grammar School	G	11, 13	45(5M)
Shrewsbury High School, Town Walls, Shrewsbury	G	11	14(5)
Hereford Cathedral School	M*b*	11, 13	35(5)
Malvern College, Worcestershire	B*b*	11, 13	12(3)
Alice Ottley School, Worcester	G*b*	11	10(3)
King's School, Worcester	B	11, 13	25(5M*b*)
Royal Grammar School, Worcester	B*b*	11, 13	37(5)
Denstone College, Uttoxeter, Staffs	M*b*	11, 12, 13	18(4)
Newcastle-Under-Lyme School, Staffs	M	11, 12, 13	68(5)
EAST ANGLIA			
Wisbech Grammar School	M	11, 13	50(5)
The Leys School, Cambridge	B	11, 13	5(2M*b*)
Perse School for Boys, Cambridge	B*b*	11, 13	12(5)
Perse School for Girls, Cambridge	G	11	15(5)
St Mary's RC School, Bateman Street, Cambridge	G	11	15(5M*b*)
Culford School, Bury St Edmunds	B*b*	11, 13	8(2)
Ipswich School, Henley Road, Ipswich	B*b*	11	10(5)
Ipswich High School, Westerfield Road, Ipswich	G*b*	11	24(5)
St Joseph's RC College, Birkfield, Ipswich	B	11	10(5M*b*)
Woodbridge School, Suffolk	M*b*	11	16(5)
Norwich High School, Newmarket Road, Norwich	G	11, 12	30(5)
King Edward VI School, The Close, Norwich	B	11, 12	18(2)
Gresham's School, Holt, Norfolk	M*b*		(5)
SOUTH-WEST Glos, Avon and Somerset			
Wycliffe College, Stonehouse	B	11, 13	5(5M*b*)
Bristol Cathedral School, College Green, Bristol	B	11	20(5M)
Bristol Grammar School, University Road, Bristol	M	11	40(5)
Clifton College, Bristol	M*b*	11	10
Clifton High School, Bristol	G*b*	11, 13	8(5)
Colston's School, Stapleton, Bristol	B	11, 13	15(5M*b*)
Colston's Girls' School, Cheltenham Road, Bristol	G	11	20(5)
Queen Elizabeth's Hospital School, Clifton, Bristol	B*b*	11	25(5)
Redland High School, Redland Court, Bristol	G	11	10(5)
Red Maids' School, Westbury-on-Trym, Bristol	G	11	25(5)
Bath High School, Landsdown, Bath	G	11	18(5)
King Edward's School, North Road, Bath	B	11, 12, 13	16(2)
Kingswood School, Bath	M*b*	11, 12, 13	6(5)
Monkton Coombe School, Nr Bath	B	11, 13	5(5M*b*)
Wells Cathedral School	M*b*	11, 12, 13	11(4)
Bruton School for Girls, Somerset	G*b*	11	20(5)
Taunton School	M*b*	11	6(5)
Queen's College, Taunton	M*b*	11, 12, 13	10(4)
Wellington School, Somerset	M*b*	11, 13	35(5)

	Boys/ girls/ mixed	Normal age of entry	Annual number of places
Devon and Cornwall			
Truro High School, Falmouth Road, Truro	G*b*	11	10(5)
Truro School, Trennick Lane, Truro	B	11	15(5M*b*)
Plymouth College, Ford Park, Plymouth	B	11, 13	30(5M*b*)
Exeter School	B*b*	11, 12, 13	25(5)
Maynard School, Exeter	G	11, 12	26(5)
Edgehill College, Bideford	G*b*	11	20(2)
West Buckland School, Nr Barnstaple	B	11, 13	12(2M*b*)
Dorset and Wiltshire			
Talbot Heath School, Bournemouth	G*b*	11, 12, 13	25(5)
Canford School, Wimborne	B	13	5(5M)
Dauntsey's School, West Lavington, Nr Devizes	M*b*	11, 13	10
SOUTH AND SOUTH-EAST			
Oxon, Berks, Bucks and Hants			
Magdalen College School, Oxford	B*b*	11, 13	21(3)
Oxford High School, Belbroughton Road, Oxford	G	11	20(5)
Abingdon School, Park Road, Abingdon	B*b*	11, 13	15(5)
School of St Helen and St Katharine, Abingdon	G	11	15(5)
Carmel College, Wallingford	M*b*	11, 12, 13	15(5)
Wellington College, Crowthorne, Berks	B	11, 13	8(5M*b*)
Abbey School, Kendrick Road, Reading	G	11	20(5)
Bradfield College, Reading	B*b*		(5)
St Joseph's RC Convent, Upper Redlands Road, Reading	G	11	20(5)
Stowe School, Nr Buckingham	B		(3M*b*)
Salesian RC College, Farnborough, Hants	B	11	20(5)
Farnborough Hill RC School, Farnborough, Hants	G	11, 12, 13	40(5)
Lord Wandsworth College, Long Sutton, Basingstoke	B*b*	11, 12, 13	12(3)
Winchester College	B*b*	13	5
St Swithun's School, Winchester	G*b*		(3)
King Edward VI School, Kellett Road, Southampton	B	11, 13	35(5M)
Bedales School, Petersfield	M*b*		(5)
Churcher's College, Petersfield	B	11, 12, 13	20(4M*b*)
St John's RC College, Southsea	B*b*	11, 12, 13	30
Portsmouth High School, Kent Road, Southsea	G	11	24(5)
Portsmouth Grammar School, High Street, Portsmouth	B	11	30(5)
Middlesex, Herts and Essex			
Hampton School, Middlesex	B	11, 13	31(5)
Lady Eleanor Holles School, Hampton, Middlesex	G	11	15(5)
North London Collegiate School, Edgware	G	11	15(2)
John Lyon School, Harrow	B	11, 13	16(4)
Merchant Taylor's School, Northwood	B*b*	11	15(5)
St Helen's School, Northwood	G	11, 12	7(3)
Aldenham School, Elstree	B	13	5(5M*b*)
Haberdashers' Aske's Girls School, Elstree	G	11	30(5)
Haberdashers' Aske's School, Borehamwood	B	11	35(5)
St Albans School, Abbey Gateway, St Albans	B	11	20(5)
St Albans High School, Townsend Ave, St Albans	G	11	10(5)
Berkhamsted School	B*b*	11, 13	6(2)

	Boys/ girls/ mixed	Normal age of entry	Annual number of places
Berkhamsted School for Girls	G	11	6(5)
St Edmund's RC College, Ware	B	11	10(5M*b*)
Bancroft's School, Woodford Green	M	11	10(5)
Chigwell School	B	11, 13	10(5M*b*)
Ursuline RC High School, Ilford	G	11	20(5)
Brentwood School	B	11	18(5M*b*)
Felsted School, Dunmow	B	11, 13	8(5M*b*)
Bishop's Stortford College	B	11, 13	6(4M*b*)
Friend's School, Saffron Walden	M*b*	11, 12, 13	20(5)

Surrey, Kent and Sussex

King Edward's School, Witley, Nr Godalming	M*b*	11, 12, 13	12(5)
Charterhouse, Godalming	B		(5M*b*)
Cranleigh School	B	11, 13	6(5M*b*)
St Catherine's School, Bramley	G*b*	11, 12	10(5)
Royal Grammar School, Guildford	B	11	20(5)
Sir William Perkin's School, Chertsey	G	11	15(5)
St Maur's RC Convent, Weybridge	G*b*	11, 12	10(5)
St George's RC College, Weybridge	B*b*	11	5
Epsom College	B*b*	11, 13	5(5)
St John's School, Leatherhead	B	13	5(5)
Kingston Grammar School	M	11, 13	25(5)
Sutton High School, Cheam·Road, Sutton	G	11	12(5)
Croydon High School, South Croydon	G	11	19(5)
Old Palace School, Croydon	G	11	35(5)
Trinity School of John Whitgift, Croydon	B	11	20(5)
Whitgift School, South Croydon	B	11	15(5)
Reigate Grammar School	B	11	15(5M)
Caterham School	B	11, 12, 13	20(5M*b*)
Bromley High School, Bromley, Kent	G	11	20(5)
Walthamstow Hall, Sevenoaks	C*b*	11	13(5)
King's School, Rochester	B	11, 13	10(2M*b*)
Tonbridge School	B*b*		(5)
Sutton Valence School, Nr Maidstone	B*b*	11, 13	10(5)
Ashford School, East Hill, Ashford, Kent	G*b*	11	10(5)
Kent College, Canterbury	M*b*	11, 12, 13	12(5)
Brighton College	B	11	15(5M*b*)
Brighton and Hove High School, Brighton	G	11, 12	30(5)
St Mary's Hall, Brighton	G*b*	11, 12, 13	10(5)

LONDON

City of London, Queen Victoria Street EC4V 3AL	B	11	20(5)
City of London School for Girls, Barbican EC2	G	11	20(5)
Forest School, Snaresbrook E17	M*b*	11	21(5)
Highgate School N6	B*b*	11	7(5)
South Hampstead High School NW3	G	11	11(5)
University College School, Hampstead NW3	B	11	10(5)
Mill Hill School NW7	B	11, 13	14(5M*b*)
Blackheath High School, Wemyss Road SE3	G	11	14(5)
St Dunstan's College, Catford SE6	B	11	25(5)

	Boys/ girls/ mixed	Normal age of entry	Annual number of places
Eltham College SE9	B	11, 12, 13	17(5M*b*)
Colfe's School, Lee SE12	B	11, 13	32(5M)
Dulwich College SE21	B*b*	11, 13	45(5)
James Allen's Girls' School, Dulwich SE22	G	11, 13	26(5)
Alleyn's School, Dulwich SE22	M	11, 13	30(5)
Sydenham High School, Westwood Hill SE26	G	11	18(5)
Westminster School SW1	B	11	8
Streatham Hill and Clapham High School SW2	G	11	24(5)
Emanuel School, Battersea Rise SW11	B	11, 13	50(5)
St Paul's School, Barnes SW13	B*b*	11, 13	15(5)
Putney High School, Putney Hill SW15	G	11	30(5)
King's College School, Wimbledon SW19	B	11, 13	16(5)
Wimbledon High School, Mansel Road SW19	G	11	10(5)
Queen's College, Harley Street W1	G	11	10(5)
St Benedict's RC School, Ealing W5	B	11	10(5M)
Godolphin and Latymer School, Hammersmith W6	G	11	35(5)
Latymer Upper School, Hammersmith W6	B	11	50(5)
St Paul's Girls' School, Hammersmith W6	G	11	10(5)
Notting Hill and Ealing High School W13	G	11	18(5)

Wales

Christ College, Brecon, Powys	B*b*	11, 13, VI	12
Howell's School, Denbigh, Clwyd	G*b*	11, VI	15
Howell's School, Llandaff, Cardiff	G*b*	11, VI	45
Llandovery College, Llandovery, Dyfed	M*b*	11, 13	4
Monmouth School, Monmouth, Gwent	B*b*	11, 13, VI	28
Monmouth School for Girls, Monmouth, Gwent	G	11, VI	13
Penrhos College, Colwyn Bay, Clwyd	G*b*	11, 12, 13, VI	12
Rydal School, Colwyn Bay, Clwyd	M*b*	11, 13, VI	7

Scotland

Pupils may be accepted for an assisted place at any stage of their secondary education. The number of places in each school should be ascertained from the individual school.

Central

Dollar Academy, Clackmannanshire	M*b*		

Dumfries and Galloway

Kilquhanity House School	M*b*		

Fife

St Leonards School, Fife	G*b*		

	Boys/ girls/ mixed	Normal age of entry	Annual number of places
Grampian			
Albyn School for Girls, Fife	G*b*		
Robert Gordon's College, Aberdeen	B*b*		
Gordonstoun School, Elgin, Morayshire	M*b*		
St Margaret's School for Girls, Aberdeen	G		
Strathclyde			
Belmont House School, Glasgow	B		
Craigholme School for Girls, Glasgow	G		
Fernhill School, Glasgow	M		
Glasgow Academy, Glasgow	M		
High School of Glasgow	M		
Hutcheson's Grammar School, Glasgow	M		
Keil School, Dumbarton	M*b*		
Kelvinside Academy, Glasgow	B		
Laurel Bank School, Glasgow	G		
Westbourne School for Girls, Glasgow	G		
The Park School for Girls, Glasgow	G		
St Columba's School, Renfrewshire	M		
Lomond School, Helensburgh, Dunbartonshire	M*b*		
St Aloysius' College	M		
Wellington School, Ayr	G*b*		
Highland			
Fort Augustus Abbey School, Inverness-shire	M*b*		
Lothian			
Daniel Stewart's & Melville College, Edinburgh	M*b*		
The Mary Erskine School, Edinburgh	G*b*		
George Watson's College, Edinburgh	M*b*		
Edinburgh Academy, Edinburgh	B*b*		
Fettes College, Edinburgh	M*b*		
George Heriot's School	M		
Loretto School, Musselburgh, Mid-Lothian	M*b*		
Merchiston Castle School,Edinburgh	B*b*		
Rudolf Steiner School of Edinburgh	M*b*		
St Dennis and Cranley School, Edinburgh	G*b*		
St George's School for Girls	G*b*		
St Margaret's School, Newington	G*b*		
Tayside			
Kilgraston School, Perthshire	G*b*		
High School of Dundee, Dundee	M		
Morrison's Academy, Perthshire	M*b*		
Rannoch School, Perthshire	M*b*		
Strathallan School, Perthshire	M*b*		
Glenalmond College, Perthshire	B*b*		

NOTE: Fifty-two additional schools will be joining the scheme by September 1989; send to the DES for a list.

Relevant sections from the Education Act 1980, the Education (No 2) Act 1986 and the Education Reform Act 1988

When writing to a Local Education Authority or a school etc., it may be helpful to quote the words of the relevant Act. Remember to mention the year of the Act and the section number, for example, Education (No 2) Act 1986, section 30.

The Education Act 1980

ADMISSION TO SCHOOLS

Section 6: Parental preferences

(1) Every local education authority shall make arrangements for enabling the parent of a child in the area of the authority to express a preference as to the school at which he wishes education to be provided for his child in the exercise of the authority's functions and to give reasons for his preference.

(2) Subject to subsection (3) below, it shall be the duty of a local education authority and of the governors of a county or voluntary school to comply with any preference expressed in accordance with the arrangements.

(3) The duty imposed by subsection (2) above does not apply –

    (a) if compliance with the preference would prejudice the provision of efficient education or the efficient use of resources;

    (b) if the preferred school is an aided or special agreement school and compliance with the preference would be incompatible with any arrangements between the governors and the local education authority in respect of the admission of pupils to the school; or

    (c) if the arrangements for admission to the preferred school are based wholly or partly on selection by reference to ability or aptitude and compliance with the preference would be incompatible with selection under the arrangements.

Section 7: Appeals against admission decisions

(1) Every local education authority shall make arrangements for enabling the parent of a child to appeal against –

    (a) any decision made by or on behalf of the authority as to the school at which education is to be provided for the child in the exercise of the authority's functions; and

    (b) any decisions made by or on behalf of the governors of a county or controlled school maintained by the authority refusing the child admission to such a school.

(2) The governors of every aided or special agreement school shall make arrangements for enabling the parent of a child to appeal against any decision made by or on behalf of the governors refusing the child admission to the school.

Section 8: Information as to schools and admission arrangements

(1) Every local education authority shall, for each school year, publish particulars of –

    (a) the arrangements for the admission of pupils to schools maintained by the authority, other than aided or special agreement schools;

    (b) the authority's arrangements for the provision of education at schools maintained by another local education authority or not maintained by a local education authority; and

    (c) the arrangements made by the authority under sections 6(1) and 7(1) above.

(2) The governors of every aided or special agreement school shall, for each school year, publish particulars of –

    (a) the arrangements for the admission of pupils to the school: and

    (b) the arrangements made by them under section 7(2) above.

(3) The particulars to be published under subsections (1)(a) and (2)(a) above shall include particulars of –

    (a) the number of pupils that it is intended to admit in each school year to each school to which the arrangements relate, being pupils in the age group in which pupils are normally admitted or, if there is more than one such group, in each such group;

    (b) the respective admission functions of the local education authority and the governors;

    (c) the policy followed in deciding admissions;

    (d) the arrangements made in respect of pupils not belonging to the area of the local education authority.

(4) The particulars to be published under subsections (1)(b) above shall include particulars of –

    (a) the criteria for offering places at schools not maintained by a local education authority;

    (b) the names of, and number of places at, any such schools in respect of which the authority have standing arrangements.

The Education (No. 2) Act 1986

REPORTS AND MEETINGS

Section 30: Governors' annual report to parents

(1) The articles of government for every county, voluntary and maintained special school shall provide for it to be the duty of the governing body to prepare, once in every school year, a report ('the governors' report') containing –

- (a) a summary of the steps taken by the governing body in the discharge of their functions during the period since their last report; and
- (b) such other information as the articles may require.

(2) The articles of government for every such school shall, in particular, require the governors' report –

- (a) to be as brief as is reasonably consistent with the requirements as to its contents;
- (b) where there is an obligation on the governing body (by virtue of section 31 of this Act) to hold an annual parents' meeting –
    - (i) to give details of the date, time and place for the next such meeting and its agenda;
    - (ii) to indicate that the purpose of that meeting will be to discuss both the governors' report and the discharge by the governing body, the head teacher and the local education authority of their functions in relation to the school; and
    - (iii) to report on the consideration which has been given to any resolutions passed at the previous such meeting;
- (c) to give the name of each governor and indicate whether he is a parent, teacher or foundation governor or was co-opted or otherwise appointed as a governor or is an ex officio governor;
- (d) to say, in the case of an appointed governor, by whom he was appointed;
    - (i) to give, in the case of a secondary school, such information in relation to public examinations as is required to be published by virtue of section 8(5) of the 1980 Act;

(3) The articles of government for every such school shall –

- (a) enable the governing body to produce their report in such language or languages (in addition to English) as they consider appropriate; and
- (b) require them to produce it in such language or languages (in addition to English and any other language in which the governing body propose to produce it) as the local education authority may direct.

(4) The articles of government for every such school shall provide for it to be the duty of the governing body of any such school to take such steps as are reasonably practicable to secure that –

- (a) the parents of all registered pupils at the school and all persons employed at the school are given (free of charge) a copy of the governors' report;
- (b) *copies of the report are available for inspection (at all reasonable times and free of charge) at the school;* and

(c) where there is an obligation on the governing body (by virtue of section 31 of this Act) to hold an annual parents' meeting, copies of the report to be considered at that meeting are given to parents not less than two weeks before that meeting.

Section 31: Annual parents' meetings

(1) Subject to subsections (7) and (8) below, the articles of government for every county, voluntary and maintained special school shall provide for it to be the duty of the governing body to hold a meeting once in every school year ('the annual parents' meeting') which is open to –

(a) all parents of registered pupils at the school;
(b) the head teacher; and
(c) such other persons as the governing body may invite.

(2) The purpose of the meeting shall be to provide an opportunity for discussion of –

(a) the governors' report; and
(b) the discharge by the governing body, the head teacher and the local education authority of their functions in relation to the school.

(3) No person who is not a parent of a registered pupil at the school may vote on any question put to the meeting.

(4) The articles of government for every such school shall provide –

(a) for the proceedings at any annual parents' meeting to be under the control of the governing body;
(b) for any annual parents' meeting, at which the required number of parents of registered pupils at the school are present, to be entitled to pass (by a simple majority) resolutions on any matters which may properly be discussed at the meeting;
(c) for it to be the duty of the governing body –
    (i) to consider any resolution which is duly passed at such a meeting and which they consider is a matter for them;
    (ii) to send to the head teacher a copy of any such resolution which they consider is a matter for him; and
    (iii) to send to the local education authority a copy of any such resolution which they consider is a matter for the authority; and
(d) for it to be the duty of the head teacher, and of the local education authority, to consider any such resolution a copy of which has been sent to him, or them, by the governing body and to provide the governing body with a brief comment on it (in writing) for inclusion in their next governors' report.

(5) The articles of government for every county, controlled and maintained special school shall provide for any question whether any person is to be treated as the parent of a registered pupil at the school, for the purposes of any provision of the articles relating to the annual parents' meeting, to be determined by the local education authority.

(6) The articles of government for every aided or special agreement school shall provide for any such question to be determined by the governing body.

(7) The articles of government for every special school established in a hospital shall provide that where the governing body are of the opinion that it would be impracticable to hold an annual parents' meeting in a particular school year they may refrain from holding such a meeting in that year.

(8) The articles of government for every county, voluntary and maintained special school (other than a special school established in a hospital), the proportion of registered pupils at which who are boarders is, or is likely to be, at least fifty per cent shall provide that where –

  (a) the governing body are of the opinion that it would be impracticable to hold an annual parents' meeting in a particular school year; and
  (b) at least fifty per cent of the registered pupils at the school are boarders at the time when the governing body form that opinion;

they may refrain from holding such a meeting in that year.

(9) In subsection (4)(b) above 'the required number', in relation to any school, means any number equal to at least twenty per cent of the number of registered pupils at the school.

The Education Reform Act 1988

TESTING

Section 2: The National Curriculum

(1) The curriculum for every maintained school shall comprise a basic curriculum which includes –

  (a) provision for religious education for all registered pupils at the school; and
  (b) a curriculum for all registered pupils at the school of compulsory school age (to be known as 'the National Curriculum') which meets the requirements of subsection (2) below.

(2) The curriculum referred to in subsection (1)(b) above shall comprise the core and other foundation subjects and specify in relation to each of them –

  (a) the knowledge, skills and understanding which pupils of different abilities and maturities are expected to have by the end of each key stage (in this Chapter referred to as 'attainment targets');
  (b) the matters, skills and processes which are required to be taught to pupils of different abilities and maturities during each key stage (in this Chapter referred to as 'programmes of study'); and
  (c) the arrangements for assessing pupils at or near the end of each key stage for the purpose of ascertaining what they have achieved in relation to the attainment targets for that stage (in this Chapter referred to as 'assessment arrangements').

(3) Subsection (1)(a) above shall not apply in the case of a maintained special school.

Section 3: Foundation subjects and key stages

(1) Subject to subsection (4) below, the core subjects are –

    (a) mathematics, English and science; and

    (b) in relation to schools in Wales which are Welsh-speaking schools, Welsh.

(2) Subject to subsection (4) below, the other foundation subjects are –

    (a) history, geography, technology, music, art and physical education;

    (b) in relation to the third and fourth key stages, a modern foreign language specified in an order of the Secretary of State; and

    (c) in relation to schools in Wales which are not Welsh-speaking schools, Welsh.

(3) Subject to subsections (4) and (5) below, the key stages in relation to a pupil are as follows –

    (a) the period beginning with his becoming of compulsory school age and ending at the same time as the school year in which the majority of pupils in his class attain the age of seven;

    (b) the period beginning at the same time as the school year in which the majority of pupils in his class attain the age of eight and ending at the same time as the school year in which the majority of pupils in his class attain the age of eleven;

    (c) the period beginning at the same time as the school year in which the majority of pupils in his class attain the age of twelve and ending at the same time as the school year in which the majority of pupils in his class attain the age of fourteen;

    (d) the period beginning at the same time as the school year in which the majority of pupils in his class attain the age of fiteen and ending with the majority of pupils in his class ceasing to be of compulsory school age.

(4) The Secretary of State may by order –

    (a) amend the foregoing provisions of this section; or

    (b) provide that, in relation to any subject specified in the order, subsection (3) above shall have effect as if for the ages of seven and eight there mentioned there were substituted such other ages, less than eleven and twelve respectively, as may be so specified.

(5) The head teacher of a school may elect, in relation to a particular pupil and a particular subject, that subsection (3) above shall have effect as if any reference to the school year in which the majority of pupils in that pupil's class attained a particular age were a reference to the school year in which that pupil attained that age.

(6) In this section:

    'class', in relation to a particular pupil and a particular subject, means the teaching group in which he is regularly taught that subject or, where there are two or more such groups, such one of them as may be designated by the head teacher of the school;

    'school', except in subsection (5) above and the above definition, includes part of a school.

(7) For the purposes of this section a school in Wales is a Welsh-speaking school if more than one half of the following subjects, namely –

(a) religious education; and
(b) the subjects other than English and Welsh which are foundation subjects in relation to pupils at the school;

are taught (wholly or partly) in Welsh.

Section 4: Duty to establish the National Curriculum by order

(1) It shall be the duty of the Secretary of State so to exercise the powers conferred by subsection (2) below as –

(a) to establish a complete National Curriculum as soon as is reasonably practicable (taking first the core subjects and then the other foundation subjects); and
(b) to revise that Curriculum whenever he considers it necessary or expedient to do so.

(2) The Secretary of State may by order specify in relation to each of the foundation subjects –

(a) such attainment targets;
(b) such programmes of study; and
(c) such assessment arrangements;

as he considers appropriate for that subject.

Section 22: Provision of information

(1) The Secretary of State may make regulations requiring, in relation to every maintained school, the local education authority, the governing body or the head teacher to make available either generally or to prescribed persons, in such form and manner and at such times as may be prescribed –

(a) such information relevant for the purposes of this Chapter (including information as to the matters mentioned in subsection (2) below); and
(b) such copies of the documents mentioned in subsection (3) below;

as may be prescribed.

(2) The matters referred to in subsection (1) above are as follows –

(a) the curriculum for maintained schools;
(b) the educational provision made by the school for pupils at the school and any syllabuses to be followed by those pupils; and
(c) the educational achievements of pupils at the school (including the results of any assessments of those pupils, whether under this Chapter or otherwise, for the purpose of ascertaining those achievements).

(3) The documents referred to in subsection (1) above are as follows –

(a) any written statement made by the local education authority under section 17 of the 1986 Act (statement of policy in relation to school curriculum);
(b) any written statement made by the governing body in pursuance of provision made under section 18 of that Act (statement of con-

clusions as to how (if at all) the local education authority's policy should be modified);

(c) any written statement made by the governing body of their policy as to the curriculum for the school; and

(d) any report prepared by the governing body under section 30 of that Act (annual reports) or section 58(5)(j) of this Act.

(4) Before making regulations under this section, the Secretary of State shall consult with any persons with whom consultation appears to him to be desirable.

(5) Regulations under this section shall require information as to the results of an individual pupil's assessment (whether under this Chapter or otherwise) to be made available to any persons other than –

(a) the parents of the pupil concerned;

(b) the governing body of the school; or

(c) the local education authority;

and shall not require such information to be made available to the governing body or the local education authority except where relevant for the purposes of the performance by that body or authority of any of their functions.

(6) Regulations under this section may authorise local education authorities, governing bodies and head teachers to make a charge (not exceeding the cost of supply) for any documents supplied by them in pursuance of the regulations.

(7) In relation to any maintained school, it shall be the duty of the local education authority and the governing body to exercise their functions with a view to securing that the head teacher complies with any regulations made under this section.

Section 23: Complaints and enforcement

(1) Every local education authority shall, with the approval of the Secretary of State and after consultation with governing bodies of aided schools and of special agreement schools, make arrangements for the consideration and disposal of any complaint made on or after 1st September 1989 which is to the effect that the authority, or the governing body of any county or voluntary school maintained by the authority or of any special school so maintained which is not established in a hospital –

(a) have acted or are proposing to act unreasonably with respect to the exercise of any power conferred or the performance of any duty imposed on them by or under –

(i) any provision of this Chapter; or

(ii) any other enactment relating to the curriculum for, or religious worship in, maintained schools other than grant-maintained schools; or

(b) have failed to discharge any such duty.

(2) The Secretary of State shall not entertain under section 68 or 99 of the 1944 Act any complaint falling within subsection (1) above, unless a complaint concerning the same matter has been made and disposed of in accordance with arrangements made under that subsection.

STANDARD NUMBER

Section 26: Admissions to county and voluntary schools

(1) The authority responsible for determining the arrangements for the admission of pupils to any county or voluntary school shall not fix as the number of pupils in any relevant age group it is intended to admit to the school in any school year a number which is less than the relevant standard number.

(2) Where any number fixed for the purposes of any such arrangements subsisting when subsection (1) above comes into force as the number of pupils in any such age group it is intended to admit to the school concerned in any school year is less than the relevant standard number, the arrangements shall have effect (subject to the following provisions of this section) as if the number so fixed were a number equal to the relevant standard number.

(3) Notwithstanding any provision of the articles of government of the school, but subject to section 33 of the 1986 Act (consultations about admissions between authorities concerned), the authority responsible for determining the arrangements for the admission of pupils to any such school may fix as the number of pupils in any relevant age group it is intended to admit to the school in any school year a number which exceeds the relevant standard number.

(4) A proposal may be made in accordance with the following provisions of this section for fixing as the number of pupils in any such age group it is intended to admit to any such school in any school year a number which exceeds both –

    (a) the relevant standard number; and
    (b) any number fixed or proposed to be fixed for that purpose by the authority responsible for determining the arrangements for admission of pupils to the school.

(5) The proposal may be made –

    (a) where the authority responsible for determining those arrangements is the local education authority, by the governing body of the school; and
    (b) where that authority is the governing body of the school, by the local education authority.

(6) Any such proposal –

    (a) shall be made in writing;
    (b) may relate to one or more relevant age groups; and
    (c) may relate to a particular school year or to each school year falling within any period specified in the proposal.

(7) If the authority to whom such a proposal is made do not give the proposing authority notice in writing rejecting the proposal before the end of the period of two months beginning with the day next following that on which the proposal was received it shall be the duty of the former authority to give effect to the proposal in the admission arrangements.

(8) Where the authority to whom such a proposal is made give such notice before the end of that period, the proposing authority may within twenty-eight days of receiving that notice make an application to the

Secretary of State for an order under section 27(5) of this Act increasing the relevant standard number.

(9) For the purposes of section 6(3)(a) of the 1980 Act (which excludes the duty to comply with a parent's preference as to the school at which education is to be provided for his child if compliance with the preference would prejudice the provision of efficient education or the efficient use of resources), no such prejudice shall be taken to arise from the admission to a school in any school year of a number of pupils in any relevant age group which does not exceed –

    (a) the relevant standard number; or

    (b) the number fixed in accordance with this section as the number of pupils in that age group it is intended to admit to the school in that school year;

whichever is the greater.

(10) Any reference in this section to the relevant standard number is a reference, in relation to any school and in relation to any relevant age group and school year, to the standard number applying under section 27 of this Act to the school in relation to that year and age group.

Section 27: Standard numbers for admissions

(1) Subject to subsections (3), (4) and (5) below, if pupils in any age group were admitted to any county or voluntary school in the school year immediately preceding the commencement year, the standard number applying to the school for that age group in the commencement year and any subsequent school year shall be –

    (a) the approriate pre-commencement number; or

    (b) the number of pupils in that age group admitted in the school year immediately preceding the commencement year;

whichever is the greater.

(2) In this Chapter 'the commencement year' means the school year beginning next after section 26(1) of this Act comes into force; and the reference in subsection (1)(a) above to the appropriate pre-commencement number is a reference –

    (a) in the case of a secondary school, to the standard number applying to the school under section 15 of the 1980 Act in relation to the age group in question in the school year immediately preceding the commencement year; and

    (b) in the case of a primary school, to the number applicable in relation to the school and in relation to the age group in question in accordance with section 29 of this Act.

(3) Subject to subsections (4) and (5) below, if proposals under section 12 or 13 of the 1980 Act (which impose certain requirements in relation to the establishment and alteration of schools) have fallen to be implemented in relation to any county or voluntary school, the number stated in the proposals in accordance with subsection (2) of section 12 (or that subsection as applied by section 13) for any school year and age group shall be the standard number applying to the school for that age group –

    (a) in any school year to which this subsection applies in relation to which the proposals have been wholly implemented; and

(b) subject to any variation made by the Secretary of State, in any such school year in relation to which they have been partly implemented.

This subsection applies to the commencement year and any subsequent school year.

(4) The Secretary of State may by order applying to county or voluntary schools of any class or description vary any standard number that would otherwise apply by virtue of the preceding provisions of this section.

(5) Subject to subsections (6) and (7) below, the Secretary of State may by order vary any standard number that would otherwise apply to an individual school by virtue of the preceding provisions of this section or any order made under subsection (4) above.

(6) An order under subsection (5) above reducing a standard number may only be made on the application of the authority responsible for determining the arrangements for the admission of pupils to the school, and is subject to the procedure under section 28 of this Act.

(7) An order under subsection (5) above increasing a standard number may be made on the application of that authority or on an application made by any other authority in accordance with section 26(8) of this Act; and on any such application the Secretary of State may –

(a) refuse to make such an order;
(b) make an order increasing the standard number to the number proposed; or
(c) after consultation with both the local education authority and the governing body of the school, make an order increasing the standard number to such number (less than the number proposed) as he thinks desirable.

(8) The authority responsible for determining the arrangements for the admission of pupils to any such school shall keep under review any standard numbers applying under this section to the school, having regard to any change in the school's capacity to accommodate pupils as compared with its capacity at the beginning of the school year to which those standard numbers first applied (whether in accordance with this section or section 15 of the 1980 Act).

(9) References in subsection (3) above to proposals under section 12 or 13 of the 1980 Act are references to the proposals with any modifications made by the Secretary of State under either of those sections; and any standard number applying under that subsection is without prejudice to the application under that subsection of a new standard number if further proposals fall to be implemented under those sections.

GRANT-MAINTAINED SCHOOLS

Section 52: Duty of Secretary of State to maintain certain schools

(1) Subject to the provisions of this Chapter, and the granting of approval to proposals submitted under section 62(2) below in accordance with the provisions of that section it shall be the duty of the Secretary of State to maintain any school conducted by a governing body incorporated under this Chapter for the purpose of conducting the school.

(2) For the purposes of this Chapter, the duty of the Secretary of State to maintain a school is a duty to make such payments in respect of the expenses of maintaining the school as are required by the following provisions of this Chapter.

(3) A school to which the Secretary of State's duty under this section for the time being applies shall be known as a grant-maintained school.

(4) This Chapter provides for the incorporation of a governing body constituted in accordance with this Chapter for the purpose of conducting any school if –

(a) proposals for that purpose (referred to below in this Chapter, in relation to a school, as proposals for acquisition of grant-maintained status) are published as required under this Chapter;

(b) the school is eligible for grant-maintained status on the date of publication of the proposals; and

(c) the proposals are approved by the Secretary of State.

(5) Subject to the following provisions of this section, any county or voluntary school is for the purposes of this Chapter eligible for grant-maintained status.

(6) A primary school which has less than three hundred registered pupils is not so eligible.

(7) The Secretary of State may by order –

(a) amend subsection (6) above by substituting a lower number for the number mentioned in that subsection (including any number previously substituted by an order under this paragraph); or

(b) provide for all primary schools which are county or voluntary schools to be eligible for grant-maintained status;

and in the latter case the order may make such consequential repeals in the provisions of this section as appears to the Secretary of State to be required.

(8) A county or voluntary school is not eligible for grant-maintained status for the purposes of this Chapter if proposals by the local education authority to cease to maintain the school have been published under section 12(1)(c) of the 1980 Act and either –

(a) the proposals have been approved by the Secretary of State under that section; or

(b) where the proposals do not require the approval of the Secretary of State, the local education authority have determined to implement them and notified the Secretary of State of their determination in accordance with subsection (8) of that section.

(9) A voluntary school is not eligible for grant-maintained status for the purposes of this Chapter if notice of the governors' intention to discontinue the school has been served under section 14 of the 1944 Act and has not been withdrawn.

Addresses of local education authorities

* = local education authorities with one or more grammar schools

Authority   *Address*

ENGLAND

Avon   Director of Education, County of Avon, PO Box 57, Avon House North, St James Barton, Bristol BS99 7EB Tel: 0272 290777

Barking and Dagenham Chief Education Officer; Education Offices, Town Hall, Barking, Essex IG11 7LU Tel: 01-592 4500

*Barnet   Director of Educational Services and Chief Education Officer, Education Department, Town Hall, Friern Barnet, London N11 3DL Tel: 01-368 1255

Barnsley   Education Officer, Education Offices, Berneslai Close, Barnsley, South Yorkshire S70 2HS Tel: 0226 287621

Bedfordshire   Director of Education, Education Department, County Hall, Bedford MK42 9AP Tel: 0234 63222

Berkshire   Director of Education, Education Department, Shire Hall, Shinfield Park, Reading RG2 9XE Tel: 0734 875444

*Bexley   Director of Education, Bexley London Borough, Town Hall, Crayford, Kent DA1 4EN Tel: 01-303 7777

*Birmingham   Chief Education Officer, Education Department, Margaret Street, Birmingham B3 3BU Tel: 021-235 2551

Bolton   Director of Education & Arts, PO Box 53, Paderborn House, Civic Centre, Bolton, Lancs BL1 1JW Tel: 0204 22311

Bradford   Director of Educational Services, Provincial House, Tyrrell Street, Bradford, West Yorkshire BD1 1NP Tel: 0274 752111

Brent   Director of Education, London Borough of Brent, Education Department, PO Box No 1, Chesterfield House, 9 Park Lane, Wembley, Middlesex HA9 7RW Tel: 01-904 1244

*Bromley   Director of Education, London Borough of Bromley, Education Department, The Town Hall, Tweedy Road, Bromley, Kent BR1 1SB Tel: 01-464 3333

*Buckinghamshire   Chief Education Officer, County Hall, Aylesbury, Bucks HP20 1UZ Tel: 0296 395000

Bury   Director of Education, Education Department, Athenaeum House, Market Street, Bury, Lancs BL9 0BN Tel: 061-705 5000

*Calderdale   Chief Education Officer, Education Department, PO Box 33, Northgate House, Northgate, Halifax, West Yorkshire HX1 1UN Tel: 0422 57257

Cambridgeshire	Chief Education Officer, Castle Court, Shire Hall, Castle Hill, Cambridge CB3 0AP Tel: 0223 317111
Cheshire	Director of Education, County Hall, Chester CH1 1SQ Tel: 0244 602330
Cleveland	County Education Officer, Education Offices, Woodlands Road, Middlesbrough, Cleveland TS1 3BN Tel: 0642 248155
Cornwall	Secretary for Education, Education Offices, County Hall, Truro, Cornwall TR1 3BA Tel: 0872 74282
Coventry	Director of Education, New Council Offices, Earl Street, Coventry CV1 5RS Tel: 0203 25555
Croydon	Director of Education, Taberner House, Park Lane, Croydon CR9 1TP Tel: 01-686 4433
Cumbria	Director of Education, Education Offices, 5 Portland Square, Carlisle CA1 1PU Tel: 0228 24356
Derbyshire	Director of Education, County Offices, Matlock, Derbyshire DE4 3AG Tel: 0629 3411
*Devon	Chief Education Officer, County Hall, Exeter EX2 4QG Tel: 0392 77977
Doncaster	Director of Educational Services, Princegate, Doncaster, South Yorkshire DN1 3EP Tel: 0302 734104
*Dorset	County Education Officer, Education Department, County Hall, Dorchester, Dorset DT1 1XJ Tel: 0305 251000
Dudley	Chief Education Officer, Westox House, 1 Trinity Road, Dudley, West Midlands DY1 1JB Tel: 0384 55433
Durham	Chief Education Officer, Education Department, County Hall, Durham DH1 5UJ Tel: 0385 64411
Ealing	Chief Education Officer, Hadley House, 79–81 Uxbridge Road, Ealing, London W5 5SU Tel: 01-579 2424
East Sussex	County Education Officer, PO Box 4, County Hall, St Anne's Crescent, Lewes, East Sussex BN7 1SG Tel: 0273 475400
*Enfield	Director of Education, Education Department, PO Box 56, Civic Centre, Silver Street, Enfield, Midlesex EN1 3XQ Tel: 01-366 6565
*Essex	County Education Officer, Education Department, PO Box 47, Threadneedle House, Market Road, Chelmsford CM1 1LD Tel: 0245 267222
Gateshead	Director of Education, Education Department, Civic Centre, Regent Street, Gateshead, Tyne and Wear NE8 1HH Tel: 0632 4771011
*Gloucestershire	Chief Education Officer, Shire Hall, Gloucester GL1 2TP Tel: 0452 425300
Hampshire	County Education Officer, The Castle, Winchester, Hampshire SO23 8UG Tel: 0962 54411
Haringey	Chief Education Officer, London Borough of Haringey, Education Offices, 48 Station Road, London N22 4TY Tel: 01-881 3000
Harrow	Director of Education, PO Box 22, Civic Centre, Station Road, Harrow, Middlesex HA1 2UW Tel: 01-863 5611

Havering
Director of Educational Services, London Borough of Havering, Education Department, Mercury House, Mercury Gardens, Romford RM1 3DR Tel: 0708 66999

Hereford and Worcester
County Education Officer, Castle Street, Worcester WR1 3AG Tel: 0905 353366

Hertfordshire
County Education Officer, County Hall, Hertford SG13 8DG Tel: 0992 555818

Hillingdon
Director of Education, London Borough of Hillingdon, Civic Centre, Uxbridge, Middlesex UB8 1UW Tel: 0895 (Uxbridge) 50111

Hounslow
Director of Education, Civic Centre, Lampton Road, Hounslow, Middlesex TW3 4DN Tel: 01-570 7728

Humberside
Director of Education, Education Department, County Hall, Beverley, North Humberside HU17 9BA Tel: 0482 867131

Inner London Education Authority (ILEA)
Education Officer and Chief Executive, County Hall, London SE1 7PB Tel: 01-633 5000 (After 1990 the ILEA will be abolished and education in London will be the responsibility of the 12 London boroughs)

Isle of Wight
County Education Officer, County Hall, Newport, Isle of Wight PO30 1UD Tel: 0983 524031

Isles of Scilly
Secretary for Education, Council of the Isles of Scilly, Town Hall, St Marys, Isles of Scilly TR21 0LW Tel: 0720 22537

*Kent
County Education Officer, Education Department, Springfield, Maidstone, Kent ME14 2LJ Tel: 0622 671411

*Kingston upon Thames
Director of Education and Recreation, Royal Borough of Kingston upon Thames, Guildhall, High Street, Kingston upon Thames, Surrey KT1 1EU Tel: 01-546 2121

*Kirklees
Director of Educational Services, Kirklees Metropolitan Council, Oldgate House, 2 Oldgate, Huddersfield HD1 6QW Tel: 0484 537399

Knowsley
Borough Education Officer, Knowsley Borough Council, Education Office, Huyton Hey Road, Huyton, Liverpool L36 5YH Tel: 051-480 5111

*Lancashire
Chief Education Officer, PO Box 61, County Hall, Preston PR1 8RJ Tel: 0772 54868

Leeds
Director of Education, Education Offices, Leeds Education Department, Selectapost 17, Merrion House, Merrion Centre, Leeds LS2 8DT Tel: 0532 463000

Leicestershire
Director of Education, Education Department, County Hall, Glenfield, Leicester LE3 8RF Tel: 0533 871388

*Lincolnshire
Director of Education, County Offices, Newland, Lincoln, LN1 1YQ Tel: 0522 552222

Liverpool
Director of Education, Education Offices, 14 Sir Thomas Street, Liverpool L1 6BJ Tel: 051-236 5480

Manchester
Chief Education Officer, Education Offices, Crown Square, Manchester M60 3BB Tel: 061-234 5000

Merton	Director of Education and Recreation, London Borough of Merton, Crown House, London Road, Merton, Surrey SM4 5DX Tel: 01-543 2222
Newcastle upon Tyne	Director of Education, Education Offices, Civic Centre, Barras Bridge, Newcastle upon Tyne NE1 8PU Tel: 091 2328520
Newham	Director of Education, London Borough of Newham, Education Offices, 379–383 High Street, Stratford, London E15 4RD Tel: 01-534 4545
Norfolk	County Education Officer, County Hall, Martineau Lane, Norwich NR1 2DL Tel: 0603 611122
Northamptonshire	County Education Officer, Education Department, Northampton House, Northampton NN1 2HX Tel: 0604 256256
Northumberland	Director of Education, Education Department, County Hall, Morpeth, Northumberland NE61 2EF Tel: 0670 514343
North Tyneside	Director of Education, North Tyneside Metropolitan Borough Council, Education Offices, The Chase, North Shields, Tyne and Wear NE29 0HW Tel: 091 2576621
*North Yorkshire	County Education Officer, County Hall, Northallerton, North Yorkshire DL7 8AE Tel: 0609 3123
Nottinghamshire	Chief Education Officer, County Hall, West Bridgford, Nottingham NG2 7QP Tel: 0602 823823
Oldham	Director of Education, Education Department, Old Town Hall, Middleton Road, Chadderton, Oldham OL9 6PP Tel: 061-678 4200
Oxfordshire	Chief Education Officer, Education Department, Macclesfield House, New Road, Oxford OX1 1NA Tel: 0865 722422
*Redbridge	Director of Educational Services, Education Office, London Borough of Redbridge, Lynton House, 255–259 High Road, Ilford, Essex IG1 1NN Tel: 01-478 3020
Richmond upon Thames	Director of Education, London Borough of Richmond upon Thames, Education Department, Regal House, London Road, Twickenham TW1 3QB Tel: 01-891 1411
Rochdale	Chief Education Officer, Education Department, PO Box 70, Municipal Offices, Smith Street, Rochdale OL16 1YD Tel: 0706 521100
Rotherham	Director of Education, Norfolk House, Walker Place, Rotherham S60 1QT Tel: 0709 382121
St Helens	Director of Community Education, Education Department, Century House, Hardshaw Street, St Helens, Merseyside WA10 1RN Tel: 0744 24061
Salford	Chief Education Officer, Education Office, Chapel Street, Salford M3 5LT Tel: 061-832 9751
Sandwell	Director of Education, Sandwell Metropolitan Borough Council, PO Box 41, Shaftesbury House, High Street, West Bromwich, Sandwell, West Midlands B70 9LT Tel: 021-525 7366
Sefton	Chief Education Officer, Sefton Borough Council, Education Department, Town Hall, Merseyside L20 7AE Tel: 051-933 6003

Sheffield	Chief Education Officer, PO Box 67, Leopold Street, Sheffield S1 1RJ Tel: 0742 26341
*Shropshire	County Education Officer, The Shirehall, Abbey Foregate, Shrewsbury SY2 6ND Tel: 0743 254302
*Solihull	Director of Education, PO Box 20, Council House, Solihull, West Midlands B91 3QU Tel: 021-705 6789
Somerset	Chief Education Officer, County Hall, Taunton, Somerset TA1 4DY Tel: 0823 333451
South Tyneside	Director of Education, Education Department, Town Hall, Grange Road, Jarrow, Tyne and Wear NE32 3LE Tel: 091 4891141
Staffordshire	Chief Education Officer, County Buildings, Tipping Street, Stafford ST16 2DH Tel: 0785 22321
Stockport	Director of Education, Education Division, Stopford House, Town Hall, Stockport, Cheshire SK1 3XE Tel: 061-480 4949
Suffolk	County Education Officer, Education Department, St Andrew House, Grimwade Street, Ipswich IP4 1LJ Tel: 0473 230000
Sunderland	Director of Education, Education Department, PO Box No 101, Town Hall and Civic Centre, Sunderland SR2 7DN Tel: 0783 76161
Surrey	County Education Officer, County Hall, Penrhyn Road, Kingston upon Thames KT1 2DJ Tel: 01-541 9501
*Sutton	Director of Education, London Borough of Sutton, The Grove, Carshalton SM5 3AL Tel: 01-661 5000
Tameside	Director of Education, Tameside Metropolitan Borough Council, Education Department, Council Offices, Wellington Road, Ashton-under-Lyne, Lancs OL6 6DL Tel: 061-330 8355
*Trafford	Chief Education Officer, Trafford Borough Council, PO Box 19, Education Department, Tatton Road, Sale, Trafford M33 1YR Tel: 061-872 2101
Wakefield	Chief Education Officer, Education Department, 8 Bond Street, Wakefield, West Yorkshire WF1 2QL Tel: 0924 370211
*Walsall	Director of Education, The Civic Centre, Darwall Street, Walsall, West Midlands WS1 1DQ Tel: 0922 21244
Waltham Forest	Chief Education Officer, London Borough of Waltham Forest, Leyton Municipal Offices, High Road, Leyton, London E10 5QJ Tel: 01-527 5544
*Warwickshire	County Education Officer, 22 Northgate Street Warwick CV34 4SR Tel: 0926 410410
West Sussex	Director of Education, County Hall, West Street, Chichester, West Sussex PO19 1RF Tel: 0243 777100
Wigan	Director of Education, Education Offices, Gateway House, Standishgate, Wigan WN1 1XL Tel: 0942 827880
*Wiltshire	Chief Education Officer, County Hall, Bythesea Road, Trowbridge, Wiltshire BA14 8JB Tel: 0222 14 3641

*Wirral Director of Education, Wirral Borough Council, Municipal Offices, Cleveland Street, Birkenhead L41 6NH Tel: 051-647 7000

*Wolverhampton Director of Education, Education Department, Civic Centre, St Peter's Square, Wolverhampton WV1 1RR Tel: 0902 27811

WALES

Clwyd Director of Education, Clwyd County Council, Shire Hall, Mold, Clwyd CH7 6ND Tel: 0352 2121

*Dyfed Director of Education, Dyfed County Council, Education Headquarters, Pibwrlwyd, Carmarthen, Dyfed SA31 2NH Tel: 0267 233333

Gwent Director of Education, Education Department, County Hall, Cwmbran, Gwent NP44 2XG Tel: 0633 838838

Gwynedd Director of Education, Gwynedd County Council, Education Offices, Castle Street, Caernarfon, Gwynedd LL55 1SH Tel: 0286 4121

Mid Glamorgan Director of Education, Mid Glamorgan County Council, Education Department, County Hall, Cathays Park, Cardiff CF1 3NF Tel: 0222 820820

Powys Director of Education, Education Department, Powys County Council, The Lindens, Spa Road, Llandrindod Wells LD1 5HA Tel: 0597 3711

South Glamorgan Director of Education, South Glamorgan County Council, Education Offices, Kingsway, Cardiff CF1 4JG Tel: 0222 44291

West Glamorgan Director of Education, West Glamorgan County Council, Education Department, County Hall, Swansea, West Glamorgan SA1 3SN Tel: 0792 471111

SCOTLAND

Borders Director of Education, Education Offices, Regional Headquarters, Newtown St Boswells, Roxburghshire, TD6 0SA Tel: 057 35 23301

Central Director of Education, Education Department, Viewforth, Stirling FK8 2ET Tel: 0786 3111

Dumfries and Galloway Director of Education, Education Offices, 30 Edinburgh Road, Dumfries DG1 1JQ Tel: 0387 63822

Fife Director of Education, Education Department, Regional Headquarters, Fife House, North Street, Glenrothes KY7 5LT Tel: 0592 727461

Grampian Director of Education, Education Department, Woodhill House, Ashgrove Road West, Aberdeen AB9 2LU Tel: 0224 682222

Divisional offices **Aberdeen City:** Divisional Education Officer, Woodhill House, Ashgrove Road West, Aberdeen AB9 2LU Tel: 0224 682222

Banff/Buchan: Divisional Education Officer, Earlsmount, Keith AB5 3EJ Tel: 054 22 2281

Gordon: Divisional Education Officer, Gordon Division, Gordon House, Blackhall Road, Inverurie AB5 9WB Tel: 0467 21291

Kincardine/Deeside: Divisional Education Officer, Queens Road, Stonehaven Tel: 0569 63671

Moray: Divisional Education Officer, Academy Street, Elgin IV30 1LL Tel: 0343 41144

Highland

Director of Education, Education Office, Regional Buildings, Glenurquhart Road, Inverness IV3 5NX Tel: 0463 234121

Divisional offices

Caithness: Divisional Education Officer, Rhind House, West Banks Avenue, Wick Tel: 0955 2362

Sutherland: Divisional Education Officer, Education Offices, Brora Tel: 0408 21382

Ross and Cromarty: Divisional Education Officer, The Education Centre, Castle Street, Dingwall Tel: 0349 63441/4

Inverness: Divisional Education Officer, 1–3 Church Street, Inverness IV1 1LB Tel: 0463 237411

Lochaber: Divisional Education Officer, Montrose Avenue, Inverlochy, Fort William Tel: 0397 2466

Lothian

Director of Education, Education Offices, 40 Torphichen Street, Edinburgh EH3 8JJ Tel: 031-229 9166

Orkney

Director of Education, Education Offices, Council Offices, Kirkwall KW15 1NY Tel: 0856 3535

Shetland Islands

Director of Education, Education Offices, 1 Harbour Street, Lerwick, Shetland ZE1 0LS Tel: 0595 3535

Strathclyde

Director of Education, Education Offices, 20 India Street, Glasgow G2 4PF Tel: 041-204 2900

Divisional offices

Argyll & Bute: Divisional Education Officer, Argyll House, Alexandra Parade, Dunoon, Argyll PA2 8AJ Tel: 0369 4000

Ayr: Divisional Education Officer, Education Offices, Regional Offices, Ayr KA7 1DR Tel: 0292 266922

Dumbarton: Divisional Education Officer, Education Offices, Regional Council Offices, Dumbarton G82 3PU

Glasgow: Divisional Education Officer, Education Offices, 129 Bath Street, Glasgow G2 2SY Tel: 041-204 2900

Lanark: Divisional Education Officer, Education Department, Regional Offices, Hamilton ML3 0AE Tel: 0698 282828

Tayside

Director of Education, Regional Headquarters, Education Office, Tayside House, Dundee DD1 3RJ Tel: 0382 23281

Divisional offices

Angus: Area Education Officer, Education Department, County Buildings, Forfar Tel: 0307 65441

Perth & Kinross: Area Education Officer, 6–8 South Methven Street, Perth Tel: 0738 38101

Western Isles

Director of Education, Education Offices, Council Offices, Sandwick Road, Stornoway PA87 2BW Tel: 0851 3773

NORTHERN IRELAND

*Belfast
Chief Officer, Education Office, Howard House, 1 Brunswick Street, Belfast BT2 7QA
Tel: 0232 229211

*North Eastern
Chief Officer, Education Offices, County Hall, 182 Galgorm Road, Ballymena, County Antrim BT42 1HN Tel: 0266 3333

*South Eastern
Chief Officer, Board Offices, 18 Windsor Avenue, Belfast BT9 6EF Tel: 0232 661188

*Southern
Chief Officer, Education Offices, 3 Charlemont Place, The Mall, Armagh Tel: 0861 523811

*Western
Chief Officer, Education Offices, 1 Hospital Road, Omagh, Tyrone BT79 0AW Tel: 0662 44931/44431

Some useful addresses

Careers and Occupational Information Centre (COIC), Moorfoot, Sheffield S1 4PQ (0742 753275)

Central Services Unit for Graduate Careers and Appointments Services (CSU), Crawford House, Precinct Centre, Manchester M13 9EP (061-273 4233)

Conference for Independent Further Education, Lovehayne Farm, Southleigh, Colyton, Devon EX13 6JE (0404-87 241)

Department of Education and Science (DES), Elizabeth House, York Road, London SE1 7PH (01-934 9000). Publications Despatch Centre, DES, Honeypot Lane, Stanmore, Middlesex HA7 1AZ

Her Majesty's Stationery Office (HMSO), PO Box 276, London SW8 5DT (01-622 3316)

Independent Schools Information Service (ISIS), 56 Buckingham Gate, London SW1E 6AG (01-630 8793)

Local Ombudsmen:

    Commissioner for Local Administration in England, 21 Queen Anne's Gate, London SW1H 9BU (01-222 5622)

    Commissioner for Local Administration in Scotland, 5 Shandwick Place, Edinburgh EH2 4RG (031-229 4472)

    Commissioner for Local Administration in Wales, Derwen House, Court Road, Bridgend, Mid Glamorgan CF31 1BN (0656 61325)

National Association of Governors and Managers (NAGM), 4 Hammersmith Terrace, London W6 9TS (01-748 2309)

National Confederation of Parent Teacher Associations (NCPTA), 2 Ebbsfleet Industrial Estate, Stonebridge Road, Gravesend, Kent DA11 9DZ (0474 560618)

Northern Ireland, Department of Education, Rathgael House, Balloo Road, Bangor, County Down BT19 2PR (0247 466311)

Polytechnic Central Admissions System (PCAS), PO Box 67, Cheltenham, Gloucestershire GL50 3AP (0242 526225)

Scottish Education Department, New St Andrew's House, St James Centre, Edinburgh EH1 3SY (031-556 8400)

Universities Central Council on Admissions (UCCA), PO Box 28, Cheltenham, Gloucestershire GL50 1HY (0242 222444)

Welsh Office Education Department, Cathays Park, Cardiff CF1 3NQ (0222 825111)

A guide to career requirements

Qualifications are becoming increasingly necessary for nearly all jobs. When you are choosing a school, the career that your child might wish to take up may seem a long way off. However, it is worth considering your child's interests, temperament and special aptitudes and finding out in advance what subjects and levels of attainment are required for a particular field of work. Some schools may, therefore, be more appropriate than others. This information may also be useful if your child has a choice of subjects, sets or streams within a school.

The following tables are designed to give you an indication of the entrance requirements for various careers and how to find out more about them. For many careers, there are various levels of entry which may vary from GCSE to a first-class degree. If you possess GCE O-level or CSE qualifications see page 33 to compare them with the GCSE requirements.

Remember that the recommended GCSE and A-level passes required for a particular career are the most *likely* requirements, not the only ones. Entrance requirements for universities and colleges usually consist of a minimum number of GCSE passes and A-level passes (e.g. three GCSEs and two A-levels). Specific subjects may be required for certain courses. The tables give *minimum* requirements only. Most university and college candidates will have passed considerably more than the required minimum. The *grade* of A-level passes is also a very important consideration. The recommended examination passes shown are, therefore, a general guide to the usual requirements for a particular career; specific requirements should be sought from the university, college or company that your child is considering.

Note that in Scotland some careers require different grades from those specified for elsewhere in the United Kingdom.

KEY: D degree required

A A-levels required (or, usually, Scottish Higher Grades)

G GCSE grades A to C required (or, usually, Scottish Standard Grades 1, 2, 3)

g GCSE lower grades acceptable (or, usually, Scottish Standard Grades below grade 3)

CSU Central Services Unit for University and Polytechnic Careers services. This publishes careers information booklets and a fortnightly national vacancy list for graduates. The address is on page 112.

COIC Careers and Occupational Information Centre (a branch of the Manpower Services Commission) distributes careers information to schools etc., and publishes career guides. The address is on page 112.

Computational/Mathematical

CAREER	LEVEL OF ENTRY	RECOMMENDED GCSEs	RECOMMENDED A-LEVELS	REMARKS
Accountancy	DA	3 including English, maths	variable	Careers for graduates are given in *Accountancy*, available from the CSU.
Accounting technician	G	4 including English, maths		Information available from the Association of Accounting Technicians, 21 Jockey's Fields, London WC1R 4BN.
Actuary	DA	3 including English, maths	2 including maths	Further information from the Institute of Actuaries, Staple Inn Hall, High Holborn, London WC1V 7QJ.
Architect	D	English, maths, sciences, arts	2 combined arts/science maths	Further information from the Royal Institute of British Architects, 66 Portland Place, London W1N 4AD.
Banking	DAG	4 including English, maths	variable	Further information from the Banking Information Service, Careers section 10 Lombard Street, London EC3V 9AS.

Computational/Mathematical

CAREER	LEVEL OF ENTRY	RECOMMENDED GCSEs	RECOMMENDED A-LEVELS	REMARKS
Building technology	DAG	4 including English, maths, a science	maths, a science	Entry at various educational levels. Further information from the Construction Industry Training Board, Careers Service, Bircham Newton Training Centre, King's Lynn, Norfolk PE31 6RH.
Cartography	DAG	English, maths	variable	Entry at various levels. Further information from *Careers in cartography*, Mr R W Anson, Oxford Polytechnic, Headington, Oxford OX3 0BP. (please send s.a.e. 8.5 × 6 in).
Company secretary	DA	5 including English, maths	2	Many company secretaries are qualified lawyers or accountants. Further information from the Institute of Chartered Secretaries and Administrators, 16 Park Crescent, London W1N 4AH.
Computer analyst	DA	3–4 including English, maths	1–2 including maths	Opportunities in the computer business are available at various educational levels. Further information from the Computing Services Industry Training Council (COSIT), 73–4 High Holborn, London WC1V 6LE.

Computational/Mathematical

CAREER	LEVEL OF ENTRY	RECOMMENDED GCSEs	RECOMMENDED A-LEVELS	REMARKS
Computer operator	G	4–5 including maths		Further information in *Working with Computers* from the National Computing Centre, 1 Oxford Road, Manchester M1 7ED.
Cost and management accountant		3 including English, maths	2	Further information from the Institute of Cost and Management Accountants, 63 Portland Place, London W1M 4AB.
Electronics engineer				(see Scientific section)
Economics	D	English, maths	2 including maths	Further information in the careers booklet *Opportunities for Economists*, available from the CSU.
Insurance	DAG	2 including English, maths	2 variable	Further information from the Careers Information Officer, Chartered Insurance Institute, The Hall, 20 Aldermanbury, London EC2V 7HY.

Computational/Mathematical

CAREER	LEVEL OF ENTRY	RECOMMENDED GCSEs	RECOMMENDED A-LEVELS	REMARKS
Jobber (in the Stock Exchange)	DAGg			No specific qualifications necessary. Opportunities for advancement at all levels. Further information from the Stock Exchange Employment and Careers Office, Stock Exchange, London EC2N 1HP.
Market research	DAGg	English, maths		No specific qualifications necessary. Entry at all levels. The Market Research Society, 175 Oxford Street, London W1R 1TA publish a careers leaflet.
Naval architecture	DAG	English, maths, physics	maths, physics	Information from The Royal Institution of Naval Architects, 10 Upper Belgrave Street, London SW1X 8BQ.
Ship/air broker	G	English, maths		Information from the Institute of Chartered Shipbrokers, 24 St Mary Axe, London EC3A 8DE.
Statistician	D	English, maths	2 including maths	Information from the Institute of Statisticians, 36 Churchgate Street, Bury St Edmunds, Suffolk IP33 1RD.

Computational/Mathematical

CAREER	LEVEL OF ENTRY	RECOMMENDED GCSEs	RECOMMENDED A-LEVELS	REMARKS
Stockbroker	DAG	English, maths		No specific entry requirements. Entry at all levels. Further information from the Stock Exchange Careers and Employment Office, Stock Exchange, London EC2N 1HP.
Surveying	DA	3 including English, maths	2	Further information from Careers Information, The Royal Institution of Chartered Surveyors, 12 Great George Street, Parliament Square, London SW1P 3AD.
Taxation work	DAG	English, maths	maths	The Civil Service Commission, Alencon Link, Basingstoke, Hants RG21 1JB can provide information about careers in Inland Revenue and the Civil Service.

Computational/Mathematical

CAREER	LEVEL OF ENTRY	RECOMMENDED GCSEs	RECOMMENDED A-LEVELS	REMARKS
Town and country planning	DA	3 including English, maths, languages, geography, history	2 variable	Further information from The Royal Town Planning Institute, 26 Portland Place, London W1N 4BE and *Town and Country Planning* published by the CSU.
Trading Standards officer	DAG	3 including English, maths, physics	2	Further information from the Institute of Trading Standards Administration, 3rd floor, Metropolitan House, 37 Victoria Avenue, Southend-on-Sea, Essex SS2 6DA
Work study	AG	English, maths	variable	Further information from the Institute of Management Services, 1 Cecil Court, London Road, Enfield, Middlesex EN2 6DD.

Creative

CAREER	LEVEL OF ENTRY	RECOMMENDED GCSEs	RECOMMENDED A-LEVELS	REMARKS
Advertising (visualizer)	AG	English, art		Art school training usually required.
Antique dealer				No minimum entrance requirements. Training often on-the-job. Further information and job opportunities are published in the journal of the British Antique Dealers Association, 20 Rutland Gate, London SW7 1BB.
Architectural technician	AGg	English, maths, a science		Further information from the Society of Architectural and Associated Technicians, 397 City Road, London EC1V 1NE.
Architect	D	English, maths, sciences, arts	Combined arts/ sciences	Further information from the Royal Institute of British Architects, 66 Portland Place, London W1N 4AD.
Art therapy	D	English, art		Further information from the British Association of Art Therapists, 13C Northwood Road, London N6 5TL (s.a.e. please).

Creative

CAREER	LEVEL OF ENTRY	RECOMMENDED GCSEs	RECOMMENDED A-LEVELS	REMARKS
Beauty culture				(See General Service section)
Chef				(See General Service section)
Dancing	DAGg			Further information from The Editor, *The Dancing Times*, Clerkenwell House, 45–47 Clerkenwell Green, London EC1R 0BE.
Drama	DAGg			Further information from Equity, 8 Harley Street, London W1N 2AB.
Dressmaker	g	Craft and art		Courses at technical colleges and training on-the-job.
Engraving	Gg	English, art		
Fashion design	DAG	English, art		Art school training specializing in fashion design usually required but some on-the-job opportunities.

Creative

CAREER	LEVEL OF ENTRY	RECOMMENDED GCSEs	RECOMMENDED A-LEVELS	REMARKS
Fashion model				No specific educational qualifications. Various fashion modelling schools offer courses, mainly in London.
Florist				(See General Service section)
Gardening				No specific qualifications necessary but GCSE needed for Park and Gardens Apprenticeship. (See also Horticulture)
Graphic design	DAG	English, art		Art school training required. Further information from the Chartered Society of Designers, 29 Bedford Square, London WC1 3EG.
Industrial design	DA	English, art, maths		Art school training required. Further information from the Chartered Society of Designers, address as above.

Creative

CAREER	LEVEL OF ENTRY	RECOMMENDED GCSEs	RECOMMENDED A-LEVELS	REMARKS
Interior design	DA	English , art		Art school training usually required. Further information from the Chartered Society of Designers, 29 Bedford Square, London WC1 3EG.
Landscape architecture	DA	English, maths, history, geography, languages	art, geography, history	Further information from The Landscape Institute, 12 Carlton House Terrace, London SW1Y 5AH.
Museum work	DAG	English, maths, a science, history	variable	Entry at various educational levels. Further information from the Museums Association, 34 Bloomsbury Way, London WC1A 2SF(s.a.e. please).
Musician	DAG	English	music	Further information from UK Council for Music Education and Training, University of Reading School of Education, London Road, Reading RG1 5AQ.

Creative

CAREER	LEVEL OF ENTRY	RECOMMENDED GCSEs	RECOMMENDED A-LEVELS	REMARKS
Musical instrument technology	Gg	English	variable	Full-time college courses and apprenticeships. Further information from the London College of Furniture, 41 Commercial Road, London E1 and other individual colleges; also consult *Careers with Music* published by the CSU.
Photography	DAGg	English, maths	variable	Varied fields of photography, including scientific, portrait, advertising, press, film and TV. Entry at various educational levels. Further information from the British Institute of Professional Photography, Amwell End, Ware, Herts SG12 9HN.
Pottery	Gg	art/craft		Art school training and apprenticeship schemes.
Printing	DAG	English, maths	maths, physics, chemistry	Further information from The British Printing Industries Federation, 11 Bedford Row, London WC1R 4DX.
Restoration	DAG	4 variable	variable	Further information from The Museums' Association, 34 Bloomsbury Way, London WC1A 2SF (s.a.e. please).

General Service

CAREER	LEVEL OF ENTRY	RECOMMENDED GCSEs	RECOMMENDED A-LEVELS	REMARKS
Advertising	DAG			Entry at various levels for executive posts and creative staff. *Working in Advertising and Public Relations*, published by the COIC gives career information. CAM (Communications, Advertising and Marketing) Education Foundation, Abford House, 15 Wilton Road, London SW1V 1NJ, is also a useful source of information.
Air cabin staff	AG	English, languages	variable	Applications should be made to individual airlines.
Army (also **WRAC**)	DAGg			Opportunities at all educational levels. Further information from any Army Careers Information Office or from the Ministry of Defence, DAR1a (officers), DAR2 (soldiers and servicewomen), Empress State Building, Lillie Road, London SW6 1TR.

General Service

CAREER	LEVEL OF ENTRY	RECOMMENDED GCSEs	RECOMMENDED A-LEVELS	REMARKS
Auctioneer (and valuer)	AG	3 to 5 including English, maths	0–2 depending on entry route	Further information from the Royal Institution of Chartered Surveyors, 12 Great George Street, Parliament Square, London SW1P 3AD. The Incorporated Society of Valuers and Auctioneers, 3 Cadogan Gate, London SW1X 0AS, and the Rating and Valuation Association, 115 Ebury Street, London SW1W 9QT.
Beauty Culture				No specific educational qualifications. Helpful information may be found in *Working in Beauty and Helath* available from the COIC.
Bookbinder	Gg			Further information from the British Printing Industries Federation, 10–11 Bedford Row, London WC1R 4DX. Fine bookbinding and calligraphy information from the Honorary Secretary, Designer Bookbinders, 6 Queen Square, London WC1N 3AR.

General Service

CAREER	LEVEL OF ENTRY	RECOMMENDED GCSEs	RECOMMENDED A-LEVELS	REMARKS
Broadcasting and television	DAG			Jobs in production, creative, executive, technical and many other fields from the Appointments Dept., BBC, Broadcasting House, London W1A 1AA or from independent broadcasting companies listed in the annual *TV and Radio*.
Butcher				No specific educational requirements. Further information from The Institute of Meat, 56–60 St John Street, London EC1M 4DT.
Buyer (purchasing and retail)	DAG	minimum of 4 to include English	variable	Various levels of entry. Further information from the Institute of Purchasing and Supply, Easton House, Easton-on-the-Hill, Stamford, Lincolnshire PE9 3NZ.

General Service

CAREER	LEVEL OF ENTRY	RECOMMENDED GCSEs	RECOMMENDED A-LEVELS	REMARKS
Catering and hotel management	AGg	English		Opportunities at various educational levels. Further information from the Hotel and Catering Training Board, International House, High Street, Ealing, London W5 5DB.
Chef				No special educational requirements but GCSEs an advantage. Information from the Hotel and Catering Training Board (address as above).
Civil Service	DAG			A wide variety of opportunities with various educational requirements. Further information from the Civil Service Commission, Alencon Link, Basingstoke, Hants. RG21 1JB.
Diplomatic Service	DAG		English, language	Opportunites in various branches. Further information from the Civil Service Commission, Alencon Link, Basingstoke, Hampshire RG21 1JB.

General Service

CAREER	LEVEL OF ENTRY	RECOMMENDED GCSEs	RECOMMENDED A-LEVELS	REMARKS
Drawing office	G			Entry usually through craft or technician apprenticeships. Further information in *Working in Drawing Offices – Engineering and Construction* and *Working in Drawing Offices – Maps, Plans and Records*, book published by COIC.
Driver/salesman	g	Maths		Minimum age 17 for driving licence.
Estate agent	AG	3–5 including English, maths	1–2	Further information from the Royal Institution of Chartered Surveyors, Careers Information, 12 Great George Street, London SW1P 3AD.
Exporting	G	4 including English		Further information from the Education Secretary, Institute of Export, World Trade Centre, Europe House, East Smithfield, London E1 9AA.

General Service

CAREER	LEVEL OF ENTRY	RECOMMENDED GCSEs	RECOMMENDED A-LEVELS	REMARKS
Farm manager				(See Agriculture in the Outdoor section)
Farm secretary	G	English		No special qualifications necessary but 4 GCSEs (grades 1–3) required for courses leading to the National Certificate for Farm Secretaries. Driving licence usually required and further information from the Institute of Agricultural Secretaries, Stoneleigh, Kenilworth, Warwickshire CV8 2LZ.
Florist	Gg			No specific qualifications required. Further information from the Careers Office, British Retail Florists Association, The Bothy, Sunningdale Park, Silwood Road, Sunningdale, Berks SL5 0QF.
Freight forwarding	DAG	English, maths, geography	variable	Language skills useful. Further information from the Institute of Freight Forwarders, Suffield House, 9 Paradise Road, Richmond, Surrey TW9 1SA.

General Service

CAREER	LEVEL OF ENTRY	RECOMMENDED GCSEs	RECOMMENDED A-LEVELS	REMARKS
Funeral director	Gg	English, maths		Experience useful. Further information from the National Association of Funeral Directors, 57 Doughty Street, London WC1 2NE.
Hairdresser				No specific qualifications required. Further information from The Hairdressing Training Board, 1A Barbon Close, Great Ormond Street, London WC1N 3JX.
Hotel reception	Gg	English		No specific qualification. Languages helpful. Application to individual hotels and head offices of hotel chains.
Interpreter	DAG	English, languages, maths	languages	Modern languages usually require additional skills. Further information in *Using Languages*, published by the CSU.
Local government work	AG	English		Opportunities exist in various fields at different educational levels. Further information from the Local Government Training Board, Arndale House, Arndale Centre, Luton LU1 2TS or your local town hall or local government offices.

General Service

CAREER	LEVEL OF ENTRY	RECOMMENDED GCSEs	RECOMMENDED A-LEVELS	REMARKS
Marketing	DAG	4 including English, maths	1 variable	Qualifications required vary. Further information from the Institute of Marketing, Moor Hall, Cookham, Berkshire SL6 9QH.
Merchant Navy	AGg	4 including English, maths		Minimum GCSE (grades A–C) standard for officers. No specific qualifications for ratings but opportunity for advancement to officer ranks within the service. Further information from any local Merchant Navy Establishment Office of the Central Council of British Shipping.
Personnel management	DA	3 including English	2	Some opportunities for those with less academic qualifications but with experience. Further information from the Institute of Personnel Management, 35 Camp Road, Wimbledon, London SW19 4VW.
Public relations	G	English	variable	Further information from the Institute of Public Relations, Gate House, St John's Square, London EC1M 4DH.

General Service

CAREER	LEVEL OF ENTRY	RECOMMENDED GCSEs	RECOMMENDED A-LEVELS	REMARKS
Receptionist	OGg			Application should be made to individual companies.
Royal Air Force (and WRAF)	DAGg			Opportunities at various educational levels. Further information from any RAF Careers Information Office and from the RAF Careers Information Service, Government Buildings, London Road, Stanmore, Middlesex HA7 4PZ.
Royal Navy (and Marines and WRNS)	DAGg			Opportunities at various educational levels. Further information from any Royal Navy Careers Information Office and from the Director of Naval Recruiting, Archway Block North, Old Admiralty Building, Spring Gardens, London SW1A 2BE.
Secretary	DAG	English	variable	Opportunities at various levels of education. Secretarial subjects can be studied at school, local authority college or private colleges.
Travel agency work and tour operators	A	English, languages		Further information can be found in *Working with Travel and Tourism* available from the COIC.

Literary

CAREER	LEVEL OF ENTRY	RECOMMENDED GCSEs	RECOMMENDED A-LEVELS	REMARKS
Archaeology	D			(See Scientific section)
Archivist	D	English, maths, Latin, French	history, Latin, French	Further information from Hon. Secretary, Society of Archivists, Suffolk Record Office, County Hall, Ipswich IP4 2JS.
Barrister	D	English, maths	variable	Further information from the Information Officer, Council of Legal Education, 4 Gray's Inn Place, London WC1R 5DX.
Bookseller	Gg	English		No formal academic qualifications required. Training on-the-job opportunities. Further information from The Booksellers Association of Great Britain and Ireland, 154 Buckingham Palace Road, London SW1W 9TZ.
Copywriter	DAG	English		Opportunities at various educational levels. *Working in Advertising and Public Relations* published by COIC gives further information.

Literary

CAREER	LEVEL OF ENTRY	RECOMMENDED GCSEs	RECOMMENDED A-LEVELS	REMARKS
Information scientist	D	English, maths, a science, languages	variable	Further information from the Institute of Information Scientists, 44 Museum Stret, London WC1A 1LA.
Journalism	DAG	5 including English unless holding A-levels	variable	Further information can be found in *Working in Journalism* published by the COIC.
Legal executive	G	4 including English		Formerly called managing clerk. Further information from The Institute of Legal Executives, Kempston Manor, Kempston, Bedfordshire MK42 7AB.
Librarian	DA			(See General Service section)

Literary

CAREER	LEVEL OF ENTRY	RECOMMENDED GCSEs	RECOMMENDED A-LEVELS	REMARKS
Public relations				(See General Service section)
Publishing	DA	English		No specific entry requirements. Varied opportunities. Further information can be found in *Careers in Book Publishing*, from the Publishers Association, 19 Bedford Square, London WC1B 3HJ.
Solicitor	DA	3 including English, maths, language	2	Various methods of entry. Further information from the Law Society, 113 Chancery Lane, London WC2A 1PL.
Teaching				(See Public Service section)
Technical writing	DAG	English, maths, a science	variable	
Translating	DA	English, languages, maths		Further information can be found in the Careers Information Booklet *Working with Languages* published by the CSU.

Outdoor

CAREER	LEVEL OF ENTRY	RECOMMENDED GCSEs	RECOMMENDED A-LEVELS	REMARKS
Agriculture	DAGg	English, sciences	Chemistry, biology	Further information from the Careers, Education and Advice Centre, National Agricultural Centre, Stoneleigh, Kenilworth, Warwickshire CV8 2LZ.
Animal work	Gg	English, a science		Various career opportunities in different fields. Further information can be found in *Work with Animals* and *Working in Care of Animals* both published by the COIC.
Archaeology				(See Scientific section)
Building trades and crafts				No specific educational requirements. On-the-job training apprenticeships. Further information from the Construction Industry Training Board's Careers Service, Bircham Newton Training Centre, King's Lynn, Norfolk PE31 6RH.
Cartography				(See Computational/mathematical section)
Civil engineering				(See Scientific section)

Outdoor

CAREER	LEVEL OF ENTRY	RECOMMENDED GCSEs	RECOMMENDED A-LEVELS	REMARKS
Coastguard				Most coastguards have previous experience in the Royal Navy, Merchant Navy or Marine branch of other Services. Age limits 24–49. Further information from the Recruiting Officer, HM Coastguard, Department of Transport, Room 8/4 Sunley House, 90 High Holborn, London WC1V 6LP.
Diver				Good physical fitness required. Training from sports diving organizations and the Royal Navy. There are a limited number of places available on a course run by the Training Division of the Manpower Services Commission.
Driver				Minimum age 17 for driving licence.
Driving instructor				Further information and training available from the Department of Transport (Register of Approved Driving Instructors), 2 Marsham Street, London SW1 3EB.

Outdoor

CAREER	LEVEL OF ENTRY	RECOMMENDED GCSEs	RECOMMENDED A-LEVELS	REMARKS
Environmental health officer				(See Scientific section)
Estate agent				(See General Service section)
Fire service	DAGg			Entry can be at various educational levels. Good standard of physical fitness required. Further information from the Home Office Fire Department, Queen Anne's Gate, London SW1H 9AJ.
Forestry	DAG	English, maths, a science	maths, geology, chemistry	Further information from the Chief Education and Training Officer, Forestry Commission, 231 Corstorphine Road, Edinburgh EH12 7AT.
Gamekeeper				Limited job opportunities. Further information from the Game Conservancy, Fordingbridge, Hampshire (s.a.e. please).
Gardening				(See Creative section)

Outdoor

CAREER	LEVEL OF ENTRY	RECOMMENDED GCSEs	RECOMMENDED A-LEVELS	REMARKS
Geologist	D	English, maths, chemistry, physics	2–3 from chemistry, physics, maths, geography	Further information can be found in *Opportunities for Geologists* published by the CSU. *Careers for Geologists* may be bought from The Institution of Geologists, Geological Society Apartments, Burlington House, Piccadilly, London W1V 9AG.
Horticulture				(See Scientific section)
Jockey				Many jockeys start as stable lads in racing stables.
Kennel work				On-the-job training. Further information can be found in such journals as *Our Dogs* and *Dog World*.
Land agent	DA	3 English, maths, science	2 variable	Further information from The Royal Institution of Chartered Surveyors, Careers Information, 12 Great George Street, London SW1P 3AD.
Landscape architect				(See Creative section)

Outdoor

CAREER	LEVEL OF ENTRY	RECOMMENDED GCSEs	RECOMMENDED A-LEVELS	REMARKS
Market gardening	DAG	English, maths, science	chemistry, biology	Further information from the Agricultural Training Board, Bourne House, 32–34 Beckenham Road, Beckenham, Kent BR3 4PB.
Merchant Navy				(See General Service section)
Police				(See General Service section)
Physical education	DAG			A recognised teaching qualification is required for teaching in schools. Teaching diplomas often required by controlling bodies for individual sports.
Sports (professional)				Special aptitude and ability in sport required.
Quantity surveyor	DA	3 including maths and English	2	Further information from the Careers Section, Royal Institution of Chartered Surveyors, 12 Great George Street, London SW1P 3AD. *Surveying and Valuation* published by the CSU has useful information for graduates.

Outdoor

CAREER	LEVEL OF ENTRY	RECOMMENDED GCSEs	RECOMMENDED A-LEVELS	REMARKS
Stablehand/groom	Gg	English		4 GCSEs (grades A–C) are required for training as a riding instructor.
Tourism	DAG	English, languages	variable	Further information can be found in *Working in Travel and Tourism* published by the CSU.
Tourist guide	DAG	English, languages	variable	Graduates should consult *Tourism* published by the CSU.
Trading standards work				(See Computational/Mathematical section)
Traffic warden				Age limits for recruitment 18 to 59. Further information is available from the Chief Constable of any police force.
Zoo keeper	Gg			Further information about careers from The Zoological Society of London, Regent's Park, London NW1 4RY. *Work with Animals* and *Working in Care with Animals*, published by the COIC give more information.

Public Service

CAREER	LEVEL OF ENTRY	RECOMMENDED GCSEs	RECOMMENDED A-LEVELS	REMARKS
Careers officer	D	3 to include English	2 variable	Further information from the Careers Service Training Committee Local Government Training Board, 4th floor, Arndale House, The Arndale Centre, Luton LU1 2TS.
Child care	Gg	English		Entry requirements vary.
Chiropody				(See Scientific section)
Dentistry				(See Scientific section)
Dietetics				(See Scientific section)
Handicapped (work with)	DAOGg			Entry at different educational levels in various fields including staff in residential homes, teachers, social workers, paramedical staff, speech and occupational therapists, nurses, doctors, etc.
Health Service management	DAG	3 including English	2 variable	Further information from the Institute of Health Service Management, 75 Portland Place, London W1M 4AN.

Public Service

CAREER	LEVEL OF ENTRY	RECOMMENDED GCSEs	RECOMMENDED A-LEVELS	REMARKS
Health visitor	AG	5 including English or Welsh		Must be Registered General Nurse (previously SRN) with midwifery or obstetric training. Further information from the English National Board for Nursing, Midwifery and Health Visiting (ENB) Careers Advisory Centre, 26 Margaret Street, London W1N 7LB.
Midwifery	AG	5 including English, science		Midwifery training for qualified nurses takes $1\frac{1}{2}$ years. Three years for others. Further information from the ENB, address as above.
Nursery nursing	Gg	English, useful		No entry qualifications required. Two-year course. Further information from the National Nursery Examination Board, Argyle House, 29–31 Euston Road, London NW1 2SD. (s.a.e. required).

Public Service

CAREER	LEVEL OF ENTRY	RECOMMENDED GCSEs	RECOMMENDED A-LEVELS	REMARKS
Medicine				(See Scientific section)
Nursing (RGN)	DAG	5 including English or history		Registered General Nurse (previously SRN). A-level standard study sometimes required. Further information from the English National Board for Nursing, Midwifery and Health Visiting (ENB), Careers Advisory Centre, 26 Margaret Street, London W1N 7LB.
Nursing (EN)	G	2 including English		Enrolled Nurse (previously SEN). Further information from the above address.
Occupational therapy	A	6 including English, biology	2 science	Further information from The College of Occupational Therapists, 20 Rede Place, London W2 4TU.

Public Service

CAREER	LEVEL OF ENTRY	RECOMMENDED GCSEs	RECOMMENDED A-LEVELS	REMARKS
Personnel work				(See General Service section)
Physiotherapy				(See Scientific section)
Police		English, maths		No special academic qualifications required although candidates with a minimum of 4 GCSEs (Grades A–C) are exempt from the entrance test. Further information from the Police Recruiting Department, Home Office, 50 Queen Anne's Gate, London SW1H 9AT.
Probation officer	DA	English		Certificate of Qualification in Social Work required. Further information from the Central Council for Education and Training in Social Work, Information Service, Derbyshire House, St Chad's Street, London WC1H 8AD and from the Probation Division of the Home Office (see above for address). Room 228, 50 Queen Anne's Gate, London SW1H 9AT.

Public Service

CAREER	LEVEL OF ENTRY	RECOMMENDED GCSEs	RECOMMENDED A-LEVELS	REMARKS
Psychologist				(See Scientific section)
Remedial gymnast	AG	5 including English, science	1 preferably science	Further information from the College of Remedial Gymnastics, Pinderfield Hospital, Wakefield, Yorkshire.
Social work	DA	5 to include English	variable	Various patterns of training leading to the Certificate of Qualification in Social Work. Further information from the Central Council for Education and Training in Social Work (CCETSW) Information Service, Derbyshire House, St Chad's Street, London WC1H 8AD.
Speech therapy	DA	5 English, maths, languages, chemistry, biology	2 from English languages, zoology, biology	Further information from the College of Speech Therapists, Harold Porter House, 6 Lechmere Road, London NW2 5BU.

Public Service

CAREER	LEVEL OF ENTRY	RECOMMENDED GCSEs	RECOMMENDED A-LEVELS	REMARKS
Teaching	D	2–3 to include English, maths	2–3 variable	Further information from the Teacher Training Branch, Department of Education and Science, Elizabeth House, York Road, London SE1 7PH.
Youth and community work	DAG	English		Entry qualifications depend on age and experience. Further information from the Council for Education and Training in Youth and Community Work, Wellington House, Wellington Street, Leicester LE1 6HL.

Scientific

CAREER	LEVEL OF ENTRY	RECOMMENDED GCSEs	RECOMMENDED A-LEVELS	REMARKS
Aeronautical engineer	A	chemistry	maths physics	Further information from the Royal Aeronautical Society, 4 Hamilton Place, London W1V 0BQ
Air traffic control	AG	3 including English, maths, science	2 from maths, geography or a science	Further information from the Civil Aviation Authority, Personnel Services (Recruitment), Room T1220, CAA House, 45–59 Kingsway, London WC2B 6TE
Airline pilot	AG	5 including Englisr, maths and a science	2 to include maths and a science	Pilots require a commercial pilot's licence. The A-levels and GCSEs specified are required for entry to the course. It is also possible to qualify by obtaining a private pilot's licence and building up enough hours to be eligible to sit the examination for the commercial pilot's licence. Further information from approved flying schools or from the Civil Aviation Authority (CAA), CAA House, 45–59 Kingsway, London WC2B 6TE.

Scientific

CAREER	LEVEL OF ENTRY	RECOMMENDED GCSEs	RECOMMENDED A-LEVELS	REMARKS
Animal nursing auxiliary (now known as a veterinary nurse)	G	4 including English, maths and a science		Further information from the Royal College of Veterinary Surgeons, 32 Belgrave Square, London SW1X 8QP (s.a.e. required).
Archaeology	D	3 from English, languages, maths, physics, Latin/Greek, history	2–3 from Latin, Greek, history, a science	Further information can be found in a free publication *A Job in Archaeology* from the Council for British Archaeology, 112 Kennington Road, London, SE11 6RE (s.a.e. please) and *Opportunities for Archaeologists* from the CSU.
Astronomy	D	3 including maths, physics, English	2 maths, physics	Further information can be found in *Astronomy as a Career*, published by the British Astronomical Association, Burlington House, Piccadilly, London W1V 0NL and from the Civil Service Commission, Alencon Link, Basingstoke, Hampshire RG21 1JB.

Scientific

CAREER	LEVEL OF ENTRY	RECOMMENDED GCSEs	RECOMMENDED A-LEVELS	REMARKS
Audiology technician	GgC	4 to include English, maths, physics		Further information from the British Society of Audiology, (Audiology Technicians Group), Harvest House, 62 London Road, Reading Berkshire RG1 5AS.
Biochemistry	D	3 from English, maths physics, chemistry	3 chemistry essential, others from physics, maths, biology	Further information from The Biochemical Society, 7 Warwick Court, High Holborn, London WC1R 5DP. *Opportunities for Biochemists* published by the CSU gives more careers information.
Biologist	DAG	3 from English, maths, biology, chemistry	2 biology, chemistry	Qualifications are at various levels, therefore entrance requirements vary. Further information can be found in *Careers in Biology* published by the Institute of Biology, 20 Queensberry Place, London SW7 2DZ.

Scientific

CAREER	LEVEL OF ENTRY	RECOMMENDED GCSEs	RECOMMENDED A-LEVELS	REMARKS
Botanist	D	3 including biology, maths, chemistry	2 biology, chemistry	A specialized aspect of biology, which can be relevant to forestry, brewing and horticulture. Opportunities in teaching or research.
Brewer	DA	5 including English, maths, chemistry	2 chemistry, a science	Further information is available from The Brewers Society, 42 Portman Square, London W1H 0BB.
Building technology	DAG	3 English, maths, a science	2 maths, physics	Entrance qualifications vary depending on the level of entry. Further information from the Construction Industry Training Board, Careers Advisory Service, Bircham Newton Training Centre, King's Lynn, Norfolk PE31 6RH.

Scientific

CAREER	LEVEL OF ENTRY	RECOMMENDED GCSEs	RECOMMENDED A-LEVELS	REMARKS
Cardiological technician	G	4 including English, maths, two sciences		Further information from The Society of Cardiological Technicians, 214 Loughborough Road, Ruddington, Nottingham NG11 6NX.
Chemical engineering	D	3 English, maths, chemistry	3 maths, chemistry, physics	Further information from Institution of Chemical Engineers, Careers Department, 12 Gayfere Street, London SW1P 3HP.
Chemistry	DAG	3 including English, maths, chemistry	2 from maths, chemistry, physics	Qualifications exist at various levels. Further information about careers in chemistry available from The Royal Society of Chemistry, 30 Russell Square, London WC1B 5DT. *Opportunities for Chemists*, available from the CSU, gives more information.

Scientific

CAREER	LEVEL OF ENTRY	RECOMMENDED GCSEs	RECOMMENDED A-LEVELS	REMARKS
Chiropody	AG	5 including English and a science	2 from maths, chemistry, physics	Theoretical and practical three-year course for examinations of The Society of Chiropodists. Further information available from The Society of Chiropodists, 53 Welbeck Street, London W1M 7HE.
Civil engineering	DAG	English, maths, physics, a language	2 from maths physics, chemistry	Further information from the Civil Engineering Careers Service, 1–7 Great George Street, London SW1P 3AA.
Dental surgeon	D	biology, physics, chemistry, maths, English	3 from chemistry, physics, biology, maths	Further information can be found in *Degree Course Guide – Dentistry*, published by Hobsons for the Careers Research and Advisory Centre, obtainable from the General Dental Council, 37 Wimpole Street, London W1M 8DQ.

Scientific

CAREER	LEVEL OF ENTRY	RECOMMENDED GCSEs	RECOMMENDED A-LEVELS	REMARKS
Dental surgery assistant				No minimum qualification although some hospitals run training schemes and prefer candidates with four GCSEs (Grades A–C) including English, maths and a science. Many dentists train assistants on-the-job. Further information from The Association of British Dental Surgery Assistants, DSA House, 29 London Street, Fleetwood, Lancashire FY7 6JY.
Dental hygienist	G	4 including English, and a science		Minimum age 17. One-year training course requiring previous experience as a dental surgery assistant. Further information from the General Dental Council, 37 Wimpole Street, London W1M 8DQ.
Dental therapist (formerly **dental auxiliary**)	GgC	5 including English, maths, a science		Minimum age 18. Two-year course requiring previous experience as a dental surgery assistant.

Scientific

CAREER	LEVEL OF ENTRY	RECOMMENDED GCSEs	RECOMMENDED A-LEVELS	REMARKS
Dental technician	Gg	4 including English, maths, a science	2–4 including English, maths, a science	Apprentices may be accepted without academic qualifications. Further information from the General Dental Council, 64 Wimpole Street, London W1M 8DQ.
Dietitian	DAG	3 including English, maths, physics	2 including chemistry, and another science	Qualifications at various levels. A basic knowledge of cookery required. Further information from The British Dietetic Association Daimler House, Paradise Circus, Queensway, Birmingham B1 2BJ.
Dispensing optician	G	5 at grade C or above, including English, maths or physics		Two or three-year course practical training. *How to become an Optician* and further information from The Association of British Dispensing Opticians, 22 Nottingham Place, London W1M 4AT.

Scientific

CAREER	LEVEL OF ENTRY	RECOMMENDED GCSEs	RECOMMENDED A-LEVELS	REMARKS
Electrical/electronic engineer	DAG	English, maths, physics	maths, physics	Those taking degrees should consult *Opportunities for Electrical and Electronic Engineers* published by the CSU. More information from the Institution of Electrical and Electronic Incorporated Engineers, 2 Savoy Hill, London WC2R 0BS.
Engineering (general)	DAGg	English, maths, a science	2 from maths, physics, sciences	Various levels of entry. Further information from the Engineering Careers Information Service (ECIS), 54 Clarendon Road, Watford, Herts WD1 1LB.
Environmental health officer	DA	3 from English, maths, physics, chemistry	2 to include a science subject	Further information from The Institution of Environmental Health Officers, Chadwick House, Rushworth Street, London SE1 0QT.

Scientific

CAREER	LEVEL OF ENTRY	RECOMMENDED GCSEs	RECOMMENDED A-LEVELS	REMARKS
Food science and technology	DA	English, maths, sciences	2 chemistry, a science, maths	Various levels of entry. Further information from The Institute of Food Science and Technology, 20 Queensberry Place, London SW7 2DR.
Forensic science	DAG	English, maths, physics, chemistry	chemistry, biology	Entry at various levels. Further information about senior positions from the Civil Service Commission, Alencon Link, Basingstoke, Hants RG21 1JB. Other recruitment information from the Civil Service Commission, Alencon Link, Basingstoke, Hants RG21 1JB.
Fuel technology	DA	English, maths, physics, biology	3 including chemistry, physics, maths	Further information from The Institute of Energy, 18 Devonshire Street, London W1N 2AU.

Scientific

CAREER	LEVEL OF ENTRY	RECOMMENDED GCSEs	RECOMMENDED A-LEVELS	REMARKS
Geology	D	English, chemistry, physics, maths	2–3 from chemistry, physics, maths, geography	Further information can be found in *Opportunities for Geologists* published by the CSU. Also *Careers for Geologists* obtainable from The Institution of Geologists, Burlington House, Piccadilly, London W1V 9AG.
Home economics	DAGg	English, sciences especially chemistry	variable	Entry at various levels. Further information from the Institute of Home Economics, 192–198 Vauxhall Bridge Road, London SW1V 1DX (s.a.e. required).
Horticulture	DAGg	English, maths. a science	chemistry, biology	Entry at various levels. Further information from the Institute of Horticulture, Royal Horticultural Society, 80 Vincent Square, London SW1P 2PE.

Scientific

CAREER	LEVEL OF ENTRY	RECOMMENDED GCSEs	RECOMMENDED A-LEVELS	REMARKS
Laboratory technician	G	3 including English and two sciences		Further information from the Institute of Science Technology, 73 Maygrove Road, London NW6 2RN.
Marine biologist	DAG	English, maths, chemistry, physics	biology, sciences	Further information from the Institute of Biology, 20 Queensberry Place, London SW7 2DZ.
Mechanical engineer	DAG	English, maths, sciences	maths, physics	Further information from The Institution of Mechanical Engineers, 1 Birdcage Walk, London SW1H 9JJ.
Medicine	D	3 + English, maths, physics, chemistry, biology	3 physics, chemistry, biology, zoology	Further information can be found in *Entrance Requirements for Medical Schools*, published by the Secondary Heads Association, 107 St Paul's Road, Islington, London N1 2NB; also from the British Medical Association, BMA House, Tavistock Square, London WC1H 9JP.

Scientific

CAREER	LEVEL OF ENTRY	RECOMMENDED GCSEs	RECOMMENDED A-LEVELS	REMARKS
Metallurgy	DA	3 from maths, physics, chemistry, English	3 including physics, chemistry, maths	Further information available from the Institution of Mining and Metallurgy, 44 Portland Place, London W1N 4BR.
Meteorology	DAG	4 to include English, maths, physics	variable	Further information from the Meteorological Office, Met 0 10 Recruitment, London Road, Bracknell, Berkshire RG12 2SZ.
Oceanography	DAG	English, maths, sciences	2 from physics, maths, chemistry, geology, zoology	Entry at degree level. Ancillary posts available for those with good science O-levels. Further information from The Institute of Oceanographic Sciences, Wormley, Godalming, Surrey GU8 5UB.

Scientific

CAREER	LEVEL OF ENTRY	RECOMMENDED GCSEs	RECOMMENDED A-LEVELS	REMARKS
Osteopathy	DA	3 to include English	2 science subjects	Four-year diploma courses with A-level requirements. Short courses for doctors and physiotherapists. Further information from the General Council and Register of Osteopaths, 1–4 Suffolk Street, London SW1Y 4HG.
Patent agent	DA	5 including English, French or German, maths, sciences	1 from physics, chemistry, maths	Minimum entry requirements are given for eligibility to sit for the examination of the Chartered Institute of Patent Agents. Further information from the Chartered Institute at Staple Inn Buildings, High Holborn, London WC1V 7PZ.
Pharmacy	D	English, maths, science	3 including chemistry and/or physics, maths, a biological subject	Further information from the Pharmaceutical Society of Great Britain, 1 Lambeth High Street, London SE1 7JN.

Scientific

CAREER	LEVEL OF ENTRY	RECOMMENDED GCSEs	RECOMMENDED A-LEVELS	REMARKS
Physicist	DA	English, maths, sciences	physics, chemistry, maths	Opportunities for entry at various levels. Further information from the Institute of Physics, 47 Belgrave Square, London SW1X 8QX.
Physiotherapy	A	5 to include English, science subjects	2 biology, sciences	Further information from the Chartered Society of Physiotherapy, 14 Bedford Row, London WC1R 4ED.
Plastics technology	DA	English, maths, sciences	maths, physics, chemistry	Further information from the Education Service of the Plastics Industry (ESPI), University of Technology, Loughborough, Leicester LE11 3TU.
Psychology	D	English, maths	variable	Degree may be taken in science or in arts/social science fields. Further information in *Careers in Psychology* available from the British Psychological Society, St Andrew's House, 48 Princess Road East, Leicester LE1 7DR.

Scientific

CAREER	LEVEL OF ENTRY	RECOMMENDED GCSEs	RECOMMENDED A-LEVELS	REMARKS
Radiography	AG	5 including English, maths or physics	2 maths, science	Further information from the College of Radiographers, 14 Upper Wimpole Street, London W1M 8BN.
Scientific civil service	DAG	4 including English, maths, a science	sciences	Opportunities for entry at various levels. Further information from the Civil Service Commission, Alencon Link, Basingstoke, Hants RG21 1JB.
Textile technology	DAG	English, maths, sciences	sciences	A variety of courses available at different educational levels. Further information from the Textile Institute, 10 Blackfriars Street, Manchester M3 5DR.
Timber trade	DAG	English, maths, sciences	variable	Opportunities at various educational levels. Careers informatiomn from the Timber Trade Training Association, Stocking Lane, Hughendon Valley, High Wycombe, Bucks HP14 4NB.

Scientific

CAREER	LEVEL OF ENTRY	RECOMMENDED GCSEs	RECOMMENDED A-LEVELS	REMARKS
Veterinary surgeon	D	English, maths, physics, chemistry	chemistry, physics, biology, maths	Further information from the Royal College of Veterinary Surgeons, 32 Belgrave Square, London SW1X 8QP.
Veterinary assistant	G	4 including English, maths and a science		Further information from the Royal College of Veterinary Surgeons, 32 Belgrave Square, London SW1X 8QP (s.a.e. required).
Zoo keeper				No qualifications necessary. A careers leaflet is available from the Zoological Society of London, Regent's Park, London NW1 4RY.
Zoologist	D	English, maths, biology, physics	2–3 from chemistry, biology, zoology, maths	Further information from the Institute of Biology, 20 Queensberry Place, London SW7 2DZ, who publish *Careers in Biology*.

Index

abbreviations 8
annual parents' meetings 95–6
assisted places scheme 12, 17, 18, 75–6, 80; in Northern Ireland 84; in Scotland 83; schools participating 85–91
appeal, procedure 22, 92; right to 22, 30

Careers and Occupational Information Centre 112, 113
Careers guide 113–65; in Scotland 83
Central Services Unit (CSU) 112, 113
Certificate of Secondary Education (CSE), comparison with GCE and GCSE 33
City Technology Colleges (CTCs) 15, 80
college of further education 80
Commissioner for Local Administration (Local Ombudsman) 23, 112
Common Entrance Examination 17
complaints 99
comprehensive schools 14
Conference for Independent Further Education 112
county schools 14, 100

Department of Education and Science (DES) 112

Education Act, 1980 9, 10, 11, 12, 18, 73, 92–3, 101
Education (No 2) Act, 1986 20, 94–6, 100
Education Reform Act, 1988 16, 21, 96–103
Education (School Information) Regulations, 1981 20
examination results 37

first schools 14

General Certificate of Education (GCE), advanced level 34, 50; advanced supplementary level 35; comparison with CSE and GCSE 33; scholarship level 35
General Certificate of Secondary Education (GCSE) 34; comparison with GCE and CSE 33

governors' annual report 94–5
grammar schools 14, 50
grant-maintained schools 16, 80, 102–3

independent schools 12, 16, 50
Independent Schools Information Service (ISIS) 17, 112
infant schools 14
Information, available from schools 19, 93, 98; available from local education authorities 20, 93, 98; the right to 18
Inner London Education Authority (ILEA) 12

junior schools 14

kindergartens 17

local education authority (LEA) 12–13; addresses 104–11

Manpower Services Commission (MSC) 80
middle schools 14, 15

National Association of Governors and Managers (NAGM) 112
national benchmarks 9, 36, 43, 51, 52–60
National Confederation of Parent Teacher Associations (NCPTA) 112
National Curriculum 96–8
Northern Ireland, information for parents living in 84; Department of Education 112

Ombudsmen, local 23, 112

parental preferences 92
parents' association 30, 63
Polytechnic Central Admissions System (PCAS) 112
preparatory schools 17
pre-preparatory schools 17
primary schools 14, 25–32
prospectus, primary school 25–7; secondary school 61–4
public schools 17

Records of Achievement 35

Scotland, information for parents living
    in 82; Education Department 112
Scottish Certificate of Education 82–3
Secondary Examinations Council 36
secondary modern schools 14, 50
secondary schools 14, 37, 61
senior independent schools 17
sixth form college 80
special needs 23
special schools 24
standard number 21, 74, 100–2
state-maintained schools 14
Stationery Office, Her Majesty's
    (HMSO) 112

Technical and Vocational Education
    Initiative (TVEI) 15

technical schools 15
tertiary college 80
Transport, right to free 23
tutorial college 80

Universities Central Council on
    Admissions (UCCA) 112

voluntary-aided schools 15, 25, 61, 100
voluntary-controlled schools 15, 25, 61,
    100

Welsh Office Education Department
    112

Youth Training Scheme (YTS) 80